The Best Book on How to Write, Publish and Market Your Novel into a Bestseller

By

Zackary Richards

Ari Publishing

4

Section 1 Where to Start

Welcome!

If you've purchased this book you clearly want information. Perhaps you want to write a novel but don't know where to start.

Maybe you've already written a book but don't know what step to take next.

You might be seriously considering self-publishing but are overwhelmed by the learning curve.

Or maybe you've already done all the above but can't figure out how to get your novel into the hands of the book buying public.

Well you've come to the right place. In this book we'll show you how to do all of those things and more!

But before we get started let's find out how many of the following standard novel writing questions you can answer?

- What is the accepted format for manuscript submissions?

- What are the 10 most common grammatical errors writers make?

- What are the 10 most commonly misused words?

- Why you don't submit in August?

- What does the phrase 'As you know, Bob' mean?

- What are the KISS and 'Pick One' rules?

- Why are contractions (for the most part) necessary in dialogue?

- What's more important: developing your writing style strengths or minimizing your weaknesses?

- How do you contact and query literary agents?

- Should you attend writer conferences if you are unpublished?

- What is the 'first 5 pages' rule?

- Should you have your manuscript professionally edited before submitting?

- Should you pitch a fiction story to an agent or publisher before you finish writing it?

- Should you join a writers group?

- Do you know the Do's and Don'ts of your opening pages and, most importantly, how to keep your readers from putting your book down?

We do. And you will too, as well as the answers to many other publishing questions once you finish reading How to Write, Publish and Market your Novel into a Bestseller.

Today's publishing environment is very different than it was only a few years ago. Most publishing houses are down to a skeleton crew while submissions continue to rise. So if you don't know the rules of manuscript submission YOUR CHANCES AT SUCCESS ARE SLIM.

Most agencies no longer accept hard copy queries. Today you e-mail your query and are told that you will get a response if the agent is interested. You could be waiting for months and not know if they even received it. Yeah, it's rough out there, but we'll show you how to stay ahead of the pack.

Traditional publishing houses no longer nurture talent or turn manuscripts over to a team of professional editors for polishing. That's your job now. They expect your submission to be a top-notch, carefully edited, market researched product before they even read the first page.

There are 2 ways to get your book in the hands of the public. Sign with a traditional publisher, or go the Indie/self-publish route. Both have advantages and pitfalls.

Let's look at **THE PROS AND CONS OF THE TRADITIONAL PUBLISHER**…

Pro: They have experience and a recognized label. They know the market and have a distribution network already in place.

Con: It can take up to 2 years before your book hits the shelves.

Pro: They know the most effective ways to publicize your book.

Con: If it doesn't cause a buzz within the first few months, they stop promoting it and move on to the next project.

Pro: They pay authors an advance. Stephanie Meyer of the Twilight series received $750,000 for her first 3 books.

Con: The AVERAGE advance for a new author is $3-7 thousand dollars. That will last you about a month or 2 and you only have 22 months to go before your book hits the shelves and four months after that before you get your first royalty check

The Pro and Cons for Indie Publishers

Pro: The author has full control over the finished product.

Con: The finished product has glaring errors and a second rate cover.

Pro: The author keeps a larger percent of the profits.

Con: Less profits to keep.

Pro: Author Amanda Hocking was turned down by every publisher and agent she contacted. She self-published and now is a millionaire, selling millions of books.

Con: She carefully researched what was selling and fine-tuned her books to appeal to that customer base.

Are you aware that of all the people bringing a book to market **the author usually receives the least amount of the profits**? For example: my first published novel, Frostie the Deadman sold for $12.95. Of that, guess what my royalty was

One dollar.

Why so little?

Expenses. It costs a considerable amount of money to launch a physical paperback book and a lot of people are involved. Copy editors, cover designers, book printers and of course, lawyers. What's more, the brick and mortar booksellers are dying so few publishers are taking chances on someone who doesn't know proper submission procedure.

Look.

When you set out to have your book published, you're essentially looking to break into the publishing business. To get a leg up on the competition (and there's a lot of it!) you'll need to know what type of manuscript agents and publishers read. And they're certainly not the ones containing those glaring grammatical or formatting errors you're not even aware you're making. Plus, if you

10

haven't taken the time to research to see if there is a market for what you've written, the odds of your novel being a success greatly diminish.

However, if you follow these instructions, you'll soon have all the skills necessary to be taken seriously as an author.

Let's get started.

In today's publishing word, authors are expected to have a social media platform, a popular blog, a professional editor to review their submissions and most importantly...

THEY MUST KNOW HOW TO MARKET!

And most writers don't want any part of that. It reminds them of some guy in a cheap suit, strong arming someone into buying something they don't want. You're not some pushy pitchman; you're a member of the arts, a novelist, a creator of literature.

But if you're not making a living from your book royalties, then that's not true, is it?

So let's have a look at the base realities. Why are you writing a book? Just to see if you can do it? Have a story the world needs to hear? Are you considering writing as a career?

Because if you are, you don't have to be very good to make money. In fact, you would be surprised at the number of 'Hacks' making a very good living with their books while real authors, (people like you who have spent years developing their craft) can't sell their books beyond their circle of relatives and friends.

What's the difference? The 'Hacks' know how to write, publish and market a book that has a built-in audience just waiting to hand over their money.

So if they're no good why are their 'books' making so much money while you, a talented and skilled author are going the starving artist route?

Take a breath, this is going to hurt.

They don't love their books. Not like real authors do. To them their books are merely a product that generates income. No different than selling used cars or pizzas. They know that writing on specific topic that caters to an eager customer base will sell a lot of books fast and make money doing it.

So what's their secret?

I'll get to that in a moment. But first, what I'm about to tell you is going against EVERYTHING you believe about the nobility of being a novelist. What I will reveal are the secrets of crass commercialism, not the art of writing, not the crafting of literature; just the plain nuts and bolts on making a buck as a writer.

So how far will you go to become a famous novelist? Ready to knock off a couple of 'penny-dreadfuls" to generate enough sales and notoriety to jumpstart your career?

Ready to dance with the devil in the pale moonlight?

If so, then pay close attention because even if you already write well and are on your way to a book contract, what I will teach you about marketing will save you months, if not YEARS of chasing rainbows and writing books that will not sell.

Okay. Here's Part One of the secret.

The reason 'Hacks' are so successful is because they study the market and find out what people are buying and want to read ***before*** they spent a year or two writing a novel that may not have an audience.

As authors we are led to believe that an engaging story, well written and well-presented will always find an audience.

That's a lovely fairy tale.

Not true, but as you're about to learn, the world sells what the consumers buy and unfortunately writers **want to believe** their first novel will be a ground breaking best seller. They tout the J.K. Rowling story, the Stephanie Meyers story, the Amanda Hocking story because people want to believe new authors regularly become wealthy and famous following the release of their first novel.

Unfortunately the facts prove otherwise.

325,000 individual books were published in the United States alone last year and that means only a very small number of authors did well.

The overwhelming number did not.

And the ones that did well were probably already well known in some manner—an actress with a children's book— a tell all book on a famous person or a well-established authors' latest release etc.

That's one of the problems with today's publishing. If you're unknown, your book probably won't receive a large enough advertising budget to generate reader interest.

In the old days if the book was good but odd, the publishing company would pour money into a lavish advertising campaign and heavily promote it in bookstores, magazines and newspapers.

Not so much anymore.

Here another fact. Many famous authors' success was due to a lucky break. For example: J.K Rowling had her first Harry Potter book turned down BY EVERY PUBLISHER IN BRITAIN, except one. And they were preparing to turn it down, but didn't because a senior executive's young daughter read it and begged her father to publish it.

Your success as an author often has nothing to do with talent and ability. Your 'lucky break' may solely depend on your own craftiness and determination to get your work into the hands of a waiting public and how quickly you can build a loyal fan base.

Section Two: Who are you selling to?

Here's a story acclaimed 'BUM' marketer Travis Sago tells his followers.

A man is trying to decide where he should set up his hot-dog cart. What's the best part of the city? What color umbrella will look best? Should he boil or grill his hot-dogs? What quality meat should he use? He asked this of other food vendors but they didn't know any more than he did.

Then he ran into a marketer who said, "It's simple. Find a large group of hungry people and set up shop there!"

Step #1 **_Before_** you start writing your book, find out if there is anyone willing to read it.

A friend was an editor for a big publishing house and he explained that many books are rejected because the marketing department couldn't figure out a way to sell them. It was too obscure a topic, or the market was saturated or the author refused to make changes that would increase its market base.

It all comes down to making a profit. There isn't a publishing house in existence that will sign you unless they're convinced your novel will make them money.

So, how do you find out what people want to buy? Simple. Go to the Google keywords tool/keyword planner and type in a topic you wish to write about and see how much interest it generates.

For example, the title of this book is *The Best Book on How to Write, Publish and Market your Novel into a Bestseller.* If you type in these words individually into the keyword box and hit Search you will see results similar to these:

How to Write-25 million average monthly searches w/LOW competition

Publish-1.5 million average monthly searches w/High competition

Marketing-68 million average monthly searches w/LOW competition

Novel-13 million monthly searches w/LOW competition

Bestseller-823,000 monthly searches w/LOW competition

There are a lot of people searching those topics on Google. How many words in your title have a comparable search volume?

In the past a publishing company would heavily advertise a book with an obscure title like *For Whom the Bell Tolls* in book stores, magazines and newspapers but today when people want something, or want to know about something, they go to Google and type in whatever it is they're looking for.

If you're a big name author, it's okay to have flowery, obscure, or just plain weird titles because readers will search for books under your name.

But you're not a big name author… yet.

So you have to manipulate the system. You put selective keywords in your title so your book title will pop up during a Google search.

Another way to evaluate your book title's market strength is to type in the keywords of the subject you plan to write about and see how much interest it generates and how much competition your book will have getting on Google's first page.

Type the title of your book in quotes inside the Google search box

This book *"The Best Book on How to Write, Publish and Market your Novel into a Bestseller"* is filled with popular keywords that will attract writers looking to improve their chances on making money with their books.

THE MOST IMPORTANT PART TO REMEMBER WHEN CRAFTING THE TITLE OF YOUR BOOK IS: ***WILL IT ATTRACT READERS***?

If the answer is no, then your road to success will be longer and harder than necessary. Remember right now, nobody knows who you are and unless you can generate interest in your book—regardless of how good it is—it will VERY LIKELY GO NOWHERE.

Keep in mind you can always become a literary masterpiece novelist and use obscure titles that have nothing to do with what the book is about *To Kill A Mockingbird* or *The Catcher In the Rye* for example) once you build a loyal fan base.

Right now finding a hungry readership is more important than your literary prowess.

Here are some Google keyword search results per month

Abraham Lincoln. Low competition 3.5 million per month

Vampire -30 million

Hunter. Low competition 30.4 million

Do you think the author and publisher did a keyword search before publishing Abraham Lincoln-Vampire Hunter?

How about:

Cowboys Low competition 6.1 million

Aliens Low Competition 9.1 million

Those numbers certainly didn't hurt the book and movie Cowboys vs. Aliens now did it?

How many book titles do you think include the following keywords?

True crime-300,000

Zombies-25 million

Puppies-16 million

Kittens-5 million

Spy-24 million

Revolution-16 million

Vietnam-37 million

Erotic- 24 million

Sex-506 MILLION!

That's a lot of hungry customers and all you need to do is insert one or more of the popular keywords people search for in Amazon and Google into the title of your book and those people will find you.

Now here are some tricks the 'Hacks' use to compile material quickly. They first research a topic that regularly generates a lot of interest. The most common are health, weight loss, self-help and make money.

Next they go to Amazon Kindle and research the sales of books that are similar to what they intend to write. They're especially interested in those with a long shelf life. It's better to write a book on a topic that has a lot of competition and has remained on the best seller list, than to spend months and sometimes years working on a project no one cares about.

You can always find a way to get in front of a large group to show off your stuff. But if there isn't an audience to begin with, you've wasted your time.

Another clever trick is to study the blurbs of the most successful books in your genre and create something similar for their own. Why reinvent the wheel when you can simply reconfigure what already works? Another important factor is they know people's interest in topics is short so they move fast and strike while the iron is hot.

To get to market quickly, they outsource content gathering to places like www.fiverr.com where for just 5-10 dollars they can get a considerable amount of research done on any topic without having to personally muddle through reference material. If you outsource, make sure they've referenced the sources so you can verify before implementing the information in your story.

Another mistake new writers' make is believing word of mouth or social media like Facebook and Twitter alone will generate enough buzz to catapult their novel onto Amazon's best seller list.

REMEMBER, the Hacks are making money and a lot of it. They understand how the system works and rig it to make it perform for them. Don't let your artistic ego con you into thinking you're above hustling for book sales.

If you've already written a novel or maybe several, and you've purchased this book to find out how to get your beloved creation before the buying public, there are two ways to do it.

You can learn the skills and tactics outlined in the following chapters to get your book in the hands of the decision makers in the agencies and publishing houses or you can go the indie route and build a fan base large enough to draw their attention by the amount of success your work generates.

Either way requires an enormous amount of time and effort.

Most authors write between five to twenty books and countless short stories before securing a contract from a major publisher, some more than that, others never make it. The media rarely acknowledges that most authors' rejection letter count exceeds the number of pages in the book they're trying to sell and that reality is FAR more common than that lucky author whose first book becomes an international best seller.

Here's something you should seriously consider doing before pressing ahead and learning the other methods to help you become a successful author.

First, become a Hack.

That's right. They're making money selling books they throw together in a matter of days. So do what they do. Put together a children's picture book, or a how-to book or a recipe book. Lay out thirty bucks or so for a decent cover, upload to Kindle, sell it on Amazon and following the methods the Hacks use see if you can turn a profit.

So how do they do it?

Here's how:

Start with a niche, meaning find a topic that people are interested in and are willing to spend money to learn more about. Choose one that is searched regularly but has low competition. As noted earlier the keyword 'novel' has 13 million searches yet LOW competition.

The most popular keywords with the highest rate of competition are health and fitness, weight loss, pregnancy, dog training and making money on line. But whatever you choose make sure there are enough people interested or you won't get any sales.

Chose 6-10 keywords or phrases that are popular with low competition

Write the book or outsource it to places like www.elance.com

Publish your book on Amazon and include the high ranking— with low competition— keywords.

Get sales because people are finding your book by entering those keywords, the more sales, the more Amazon helps promote your book. Remember the higher you rank the more sales you'll get.

Then do it again by creating additional quickly written books until all your 'Hack' books are selling well. Now that you know how to market your books, this is the time to start reconfiguring your novels into those that sell.

Another way is to take a popular and highly competitive niche and drill down to a specific category.

For example: Pregnancy

Go to www.Amazon.com and under books in the search bar, type in pregnancy. Once done, on the left you will see a listing of categories. Choose one: For example 'Pregnancy and Childbirth'. Click on that and you will be led to a sub category with additional topics, click on Woman's health and that will take you to another subcategory where we chose Sexual health where there is only 11 book titles. Copy the URL of the top website and place it into www.Quantcast.com to find out the demographics of the people reading those books

You will have no trouble getting to the top of the Google and Amazon search engines with so little competition.

Take the time to learn from those who have already succeeded. Purchase and download books from marketers who explain in detail exactly how they maneuvered their 'How to be a Kindle best seller' e books to the top of the Google and Amazon Kindle pages.

Go to the library and get audio books on marketing.

Read the blogs of authors who have achieved online success with their books (Amanda Hocking, J. A. Konrath)

Throughout history we've seen musicians, writers and artists seeking patrons to subsidize their work. Because of internet marketing that's no longer necessary. We can finance and promote our own work. We're smart, talented and creative and don't need some publisher to pay for the construction and distribution of physical books.

Hardcover and paperback books are going the way of vinyl records and 8 track tapes. Frankly, we don't need mainstream publishers at all.

However, if you're determined to be signed by some big publishing house and enjoy a career like J.K. Rowling or John Grisham, but don't quite know how to go about it or what skills you'll need to be taken seriously, you've come to the right place because I'm going to show you how to create a novel the professionals want to read.

Section 3 -The Basics

We'll begin with the very basics on format and submission policy for mainstream publishing houses and literary agencies. Although acceptance policy varies, I'll show you the most conservative format, one accepted by all agents and publishers. I suggest you take notes. It is likely you will come upon some technique that you'll want to incorporate into your writing. Write them down now so you won't have to skip around this book while reading a later section.

If you are already familiar with Microsoft WORD setup, you can skip to the next section.

First, use Microsoft Word. Everybody uses it, and it's easy to forward as an attachment. You don't want your book being passed over because of incompatible software. In addition you won't have problems with conversion should you go the indie route and want to create an e book.

Seriously, there's a Microsoft WORD version for Macs. Install that program and save yourself some grief down the road.

The default page size for Microsoft WORD is standard letter size 8.5''x 11'' This size is considered the standard for manuscript submissions. If for some reason this is not the default on your machine you can change it by clicking on the Page Layout on the top toolbar

Directly below, click on the SIZE icon. A drop down menu will appear. Check to see if it contains LETTER 8.5"x11" of so click that box. If not go the bottom, click on the box that reads: MORE PAPER SIZES. A new box will appear. Fill in 8.5 in the width box. Fill in 11 in the height box. Then go to the bottom click OK and you're all set.

Next. Go to the top toolbar, left side, click on HOME.

Directly under the words PAGE LAYOUT is a box with a drop down menu. Click on the arrow, scroll down to Times New Roman which is the font I'm using for this book and click it. The word Times New Roman should appear in the box. There are other acceptable fonts but this is the most common and unlikely to cause any reader grief.

Next to that box is the font size. The acceptable sizes are 12 and 14. I chose 14 because it's a little larger than standard 12 but easier to read. Either is acceptable.

Next. Although all books are single spaced, **manuscripts must be DOUBLE SPACED.** This is so there is room for notes and corrections.

Note: Directly below the top toolbar is another with 5 units, their names are at the bottom. The first is CLIPBOARD, the 2nd FONT, the 3rd PARAGRAPH the 4th STYLES and the 5th EDITING.

You'll notice the first 4 have a little arrow at the bottom right corner. Go to Paragraph and click that arrow.

A drop down box will appear. Here what to do with each drop down box. Under Alignment: Click on the arrow and chose Justified. The name Justified should appear in the box. Under OUTLINE LEVEL should be the word Body Text. If not, click on the arrow and select it.

Under INDENTATION both left and right boxes should read 0

In the box marked SPECIAL click on the arrow and choose FIRST LINE

In the box marked BY: chose the number 3. I know the default is 5 and many people use that but 3 works just as well and is the preferred indent for Kindle and Nook.

Under SPACING the box marked BEFORE should be 0

The box marked <u>AFTER</u> should read 10

To the right under <u>LINE SPACING</u> click on the arrow and chose *DOUBLE*

Leave the <u>AT</u>: box blank

Then click on the box that reads **<u>DON'T AD SPACE BETWEEN PARAGRAPHs OF THE SAME STYLE</u>**.

It is important that you click this box because if you don't every paragraph will be separated by a space, which will confuse the reader because a space after a paragraph usually means a jump cut in a novel (a jump cut indicates a scene change, but more on that later) Note* It is okay to use the paragraph separator for tutorials or how-to's (like this book for example)

Next. Scroll down to OK and click.

Now you need to do just two more things.

Go to the top tool bar and click on Insert. In the 5th unit across on the right you'll see the Header and Footer unit. Click on the Header icon.

Next, in the top box fill in the title of your book followed by/your name.

For example, if this were a novel I'd type in The Best Book on How to Write, Publish and Market your Novel into a Bestseller/Zackary Richards

Once done, go to the right of the toolbar and click close Header and Footer. That will place the title of your book and your name on the top left hand side of the page.

Next, go to top toolbar again. Click on Insert. This time in the Footer box click on page number. The drop down menu will appear. Click on BOTTOM OF PAGE. Another drop down menu will appear. Click on the 2nd one down where the number 1 is in the center

The reason for adding Headers and Page Numbers is because you will submit your double spaced properly formatted manuscript with no staples or bindings. (DO NOT punch holes in it and put it in a binder.) And should the agent, publisher or editor accidently drop your manuscript, having page numbers will make it possible to reassemble and the name and author at the top left will also help should your manuscript get accidently mixed in with someone else's.

I usually place my manuscript in between two pieces of firm but thin cardboard cut to the size of the manuscript. Then wrap two thick rubber bands around it, placed it in a box or strong envelope and send it out.

Let's Talk about Rookie Mistakes

Villain # 1 Exposition. Exposition is where an important part of back-story is revealed. The trick is to REVEAL THE STORY without stopping the action.

In this example an elderly dementia patient is being cared for by his adult daughter. In this scene she is sitting in her old bedroom and lamenting her situation.

"How on Earth did I wind up back in my old bedroom in my parent's house? Sure, it's nice and has plenty of room but I'm the freakin' executive vice president of the Goldenrod Hotel chain! I make enough money to buy this house and every house on this block! So why am I living with my father?"

As you can see, the action during that monologue stopped dead as the information dump truck did its business.

A better way would be for her to receive a phone call from her boss, and in that conversation, reveal that same information in a heated discussion.

For example, her cell phone rings. She reads the number. "Oh crap! I told him I was taking this week off, what the hell does he want?" She takes the call.

A moment later she rolls her eyes. "Well I can't help you with that, Elliot. I told you I was taking care of my father this week. What? No don't give me that, 'you have important responsibilities as the executive VP of the Goldenrod Hotel Chain,' crap! I am well aware of my responsibilities."

She again rolls her eyes and shakes her head and begins pacing. "Look I'm sorry, but I gave you more than ample time to rearrange your schedule and if you didn't well, that's on you. I have to go; I'll talk to you Monday."

As she ends the call her sister sticks her head in and says, "Trouble at work?"

She replies, "There better not be, because if he gives me grief, I'll quit, buy the controlling shares of our competitor and drive that idiot out of business."

In the second version, the same information was presented, but in a more interesting manner.

Rookie mistake #2 Writing in the passive voice

The passive voice makes for a boring read. Here's is an example of the passive voice "We were invited to a party by our neighbors." The active voice would be "Our neighbors invited us to a party."

Passive voice: "Joan was verbally abused by the critics."

Active voice: The critics verbally abused Joan."

There is a fun trick that tells if your sentence is in the active or passive voice. After the verb, insert the words 'by zombies'. If the sentence makes some sense you're in the passive voice. If not, you're in the active. Let's take another look at the examples

"We were invited (by zombies)… makes sense so it's passive voice

Our neighbors invited (by zombies)… make no sense so it's active voice.

Let's look at the second example

Joan was verbally abused (by zombies)… makes sense, so passive voice

The critics verbally abused (by zombies)… make no sense, so active voice

Another tip* When you reach the end of a chapter, don't scroll down to the next blank page. This will cause problems down the road when you upload to Kindle. When you get to the end of a chapter, go to the top toolbar, click on INSERT.

Then in the pages box (It's the first one on the left,) click on page break.

Two more helpful hints. When you write your first draft, don't number your chapters. At the beginning of each chapter, simply write the word CHAPTER at the top. Why? Because during the creation of a novel things change, timelines change, you may have to move people and scenes around.

You don't want to be wasting time adjusting chapter numbers when you're knee deep in an important scene. You can add chapter numbers when the book is completed.

Next, create a scrap file for your book. I've learned that I sometimes write scenes out of sync. What I mean is I'll be writing a storyline and then discover 5 or 6 pages in, that it's leading nowhere.

Don't delete it. Simply cut and paste it to your scrap file. On many occasions I've found that parts I removed because the storyline wasn't working earlier in the book fit in perfectly in later chapters. Having a scrap file saved me considerable rewriting time.

Section 4-The Initial approach

Fiction and non-fiction writers should approach their writing in a manner that best suits their craft. For non-fiction writers now is the time to gather information. Once done, create sections on a timeline in which that data will be revealed to your reader.

For example, if you're writing a book on playing guitar, your first chapter will likely be about stringing and tuning, the next, simple strumming techniques. The third, basic chords and so on.

If writing a historical novel on George Washington, compile the data then write the story revealing your specific view of the man from his birth to his death.

Writing fiction is different. First, you must find out if you have a story. And the only way to find out of you have a story is to write one.

Write the complete first draft.

I am the moderator of a writers group. Every two weeks we get together to edit and critique each other's work in the hope of finding ways to improve it.

One problem I consistently see is novice writers entangling themselves in the PROCESS of writing. Before they actually begin their stories, they create extensive outlines, write full biographies of their characters, investigate the weather patterns of the places they're going to write about, and create psychological profiles of their antagonists.

On and on it goes. The actual writing they produce however is minimal. They set writing goals they never achieve, abandon projects they barely started, then enthusiastically start a new one and immediately fall into the same unproductive pattern.

Writers, write. If you're formulating a complex novel, some preparation and research will be necessary, but only enough to get you started.

Then you write and you write every day.

Every day. You don't stop to edit, or focus on getting the exact right word, or look up proper spelling, or check to see what the capitol of Jamaica is, you just write. And if you can't think of what to write then write about your characters, their morning routine, what are they wearing, what they eat for breakfast, and do they have to bring their car to the shop for service? Is there an outstanding bill that needs to be paid?

This is an opportunity for us, the readers, get to know your character's better.

Doing that will prime the pump, the juices will kick in and you'll be back working on your story in no time.

The inimitable Dorothy Parker once said: "I hate writing, but I love having written."

Admittedly, writing is tough but there are tricks to get things in motion. For example, if I find the project I'm working on becoming a chore, I'll start a second project, and if that peters out I'll open a third. But that's as far as I'll go. Then each day I'll sit down and spend a minimum of 4 hours working on one of those 3 projects. Usually it's the one I hate the least. Eventually one of them will kick into high gear and that's the book I'll devote all my attention to and finish.

That keeps me writing every day.

Leonard Nimoy once said, "Directing a movie is like eating an elephant. The enormousness of the project is staggering but if you eat some of the elephant each and every day, eventually the elephant will be gone. So don't be afraid of taking on big projects. If you are persistent, you will complete it.

Okay, you've started writing regularly. Got some short stories under your belt and are several chapters into your first full length novel. What do you do now? You take the next step. You join a writers group. There you'll find people with more experience, who, if you ask nicely, will help you with writing tips and advice. As your skills improve, take classes. Then put that information into practice because the ONLY way to develop your talent and hone your skills is by USING them.

And by taking these steps there's something else you'll learn.

You'll learn how talented and how committed you really are and if your stories are consistently improving then don't let anyone stop you.

Now let's talk about pacing. This is important because without variations in pacing, your novel will read like someone singing in monotone. It will drone on and on and accomplish nothing. You have to shift gears throughout your novel to keep your readers interested.

Alfred Hitchcock the director was famous for this. He'd rev up the tension and suspense to a fever pitch and just when you think you're going to burst... he'd throw in a joke and everyone would be stunned and more importantly greatly amused.

This works for the same reason a roller-coaster works. It slowly clickity-clacks upward building the suspense, one second after another until, you reach the very top, then BOOM you're rocketing downward at breakneck speed. You're thrown wildly from side to side, then upside down, then in the dark. Your heart is pounding, your eyes widening, you can't catch your breath but you're having the time of your life…

Then it's over.

And you want to do it again!

That's what your writing needs to do. Your goal, regardless of style, is to have your readers WANT to ride with you again.

Do the unexpected. No one enjoys a predictable novel. Be courageous, take chances and should your novel fall apart, then accept the fact that it wasn't very good to begin with and start something new.

In my books I envision seeing you in a dark and dangerous neighborhood. There is a group of trouble-makers approaching you, shouting threats. I pull my car alongside, screech to a stop, fling open the car door, and shout, "Get in!" You comply and I burn rubber down the street.

Days later, having shared an incredible adventure, I drop you at your place. As you step outside and are about to close the door, you lean in and say, "Next time before you head out, come and get me."

Damn right I will!

Here's some tricks to vary your pacing. When you want to build suspense, fill the scene with minute detail. Describe the room, its furnishings, what's on the walls.

Then ratchet up the tension with mysterious sounds, like the low moan of the winds as they race through the barren trees, sights, like a rat sprinting alongside the floorboards, smells, like the harsh scent of rotting blood that grows stronger with each step.

The floor creaks; a sudden breeze slams a door. You hear a sound, a whisper? A child's voice? No. Yes? You hear a something breathing several steps behind you, your body stiffens, your heart pounds. You turn, but there's no one there.

Or is there?

The heavy maroon curtain moves ever so slightly. After several deep breaths, you steel your nerves and cautiously approach. You reach out your hand, it's shaking, your breath is in short gasps. You grip the curtain and yank it open. A dark figure leaps toward you. You jerk backward with hands raised in panic…

…as the cat lands on the floor and scurries down the hall.

Typical Hitchcock.

Action scenes are the exact opposite and should be cut to the bare essentials because the readers need to keep pace with the action.

Here's an example:

Four gun shots rang out. Splinters flew and bullets ricocheted as Jake ran toward the horse stalls. A bullet grazed his shoulder as he vaulted head first over the gate. Two more ripped into the wooden post behind him

Banshee, frightened by the thunderous gunfire had reared up in panic.

As Jake tumbled across the stall's hay covered floor, his eyes widened when he saw the mighty steed's hooves racing toward him. He jerked to his side as they slammed down, just inches away. He grabbed Banshee's leg as the horse reared a second time. Now on his feet, Jake pulled his gun.

A flash of light. The stall slat beside his face exploded, splinters flew in all directions. Jake fired.

Blood splattered against the barn door.

Action scene should be set like dominoes. You build tension and suspense by setting a detailed scene then the action begins as the dominoes fall. Since you've already set the scene, additional details are unnecessary and will slow the pace.

So keep it tight.

Another way to keep your readers engaged is to omit words regularly used in conversation but have no place in a novel. For example: "He decided that he'd take the bus." The word 'that' is unnecessary. The sentence, "He decided he'd take the bus." is better without it. The word 'that' is often added out of habit. Take it out wherever it adds nothing to the sentence.

The words Up and Down should be checked and mainly used when indicating direction. For example: *He sat down on the couch.* In that sentence the word down is unnecessary. *He sat on the couch.* is better.

Another example: He had been feeling lonely without her. Replace HAD BEEN FEELING with was. He <u>was</u> lonely without her.

Perhaps the most unnecessary word is the begin/began combo. Take the sentence: "He began thinking about the time they went sailing. Replace 'began thinking about' with thought. As in: He thought about the time they went sailing.

Another group to omit is unnecessary words and lead in phrases. Sentences that lead with:

The point is

First of all

So

Anyway

You see

You need to know

In most cases

This is not to say they all must be removed. I often use 'Anyway' as a lead-in word because it fits my writing style.

Anyway...

Omitting unnecessary words doesn't take from or change your writer's voice, it keeps you and your readers from slogging through meaningless words and phrases that add nothing and in most case slow the pacing (Thought I was going to say slow the pacing down, didn't you?)

There are always exceptions but I stand by my position. If a word or phrase adds nothing to the sentence, remove it.

Remember we're not selling donuts here. Additional words do not make a better product. Strong, concise to-the–point words do.

Let's talk about your strengths. Once you're writing regularly you'll notice you do some things better than others. I do action/adventure well. I struggle with romance scenes.

A woman in my writers group has a remarkable ability to describe the places she's been in such poetic detail you feel you're actually there.

Some places are wildly exotic, some as common as a factory in a warehouse district, either way you're right beside her. You can smell the exotic fragrances from foreign shores as the two of you float gently down a tropical river.

The next day you smell the burnt oil from the factory machines as you both work on the assembly line. Her stories aren't all that interesting, but I don't read them for the stories. I read them for the places she takes me. At the end of each one I say to her, "Before you head out the next time, come and get me."

She always does.

Once your strengths are revealed, work on them; push that talent as far as it will go. A top-notch baseball pitcher doesn't work on hitting home runs. He works on perfecting his pitching, just as the long ball hitter concentrates on hitting.

Don't waste time trying to build your weaknesses. Learn the skills necessary to do the job, then get right back to your bread and butter. Find out what you do well and learn to do it better and keep at it until you're the best!

Now let's discuss the jump cut.

The jump cut is when you place a noticeable space between two paragraphs. If, in your story, there is a dull part that is not essential, do a jump cut to the part when the story becomes interesting again.

Here's an example.

Bob jumped out of bed six times that night. Just as he was about to drift off to sleep, he'd experience sudden excruciating pain from the tooth he had broken just before going to bed. Come morning he made an emergency appointment with his dentist Dr. Sugarman who agreed to see him right away. Nodding in relief, Bob ended the call and raced to his car.

So Bob got into his car, started the engine, pulled out of the driveway and backed into the street. After turning the wheel in the proper direction, he pressed the accelerator and his BMW took off. When he arrived at the corner he waited for the light to change then made a turn on Sullivan Street which led to Dr. Sugarman's office, a half mile away.

Are you falling asleep yet?

Who cares about Bob's drive to the dentist's office? It has nothing to do with the story, and certainly doesn't entertain the reader so why is it there?

It shouldn't be.

After the part where Dr. Sugarman agrees to see Bob right away, you should insert a space between the paragraphs. At the beginning of the next paragraph, write something like:

Fifteen minutes later, Bob rushed into Dr. Sugarman's reception area holding the side of his face.

If you want to change scenes but don't want to start a new chapter, insert a jump cut and place an asterisk *, or squiggly line ~~ in the center between the two paragraphs. For example:

Come morning he made an emergency appointment with his dentist Dr. Sugarman who agreed to see him right away. Nodding in relief, Bob ended the call and raced to his car.

*

Five years ago Bob's wife Jane would have accompanied him. Nowadays she didn't care if his head blew off. As she watched him drive away…
Then when you're done with Jane and want to go back to Bob's story, you do another jump cut throw in a separator and pick up where you left off.

Section 5-Basic grammar.

Although it is not necessary to have a Master of Fine Arts degree to create an acceptable manuscript, you must know the basics if you want to be taken seriously.

Many publishing houses have college students as interns. Their job is to go through the slush piles (which are manuscripts sent in without being requested) and eliminate those poorly written or uninteresting.

Remember these interns are looking to get hired and desperately want to impress the higher-ups. They're not going to forward a manuscript filled with common errors because that would suggest they don't know what those errors are. Here's a list of the most common.

First: In dialogue, don't follow an exclamation point or question mark with a capital letter unless you're starting a new sentence.

For example:

Incorrect: "Stop yelling at me!" <u>Sh</u>e said.

Correct: "Stop yelling at me!" <u>sh</u>e said.

Although your spell check might underline the <u>she</u> in the second sentence, it is correct.

The same goes for a question.

For example:

Incorrect: "Do you have my car keys?" She asked

Correct: "Do you have my car keys?" she asked.

Next is the correct usage of there, their & they're

There indicates place. "My car is over <u>there</u>."

Their indicates ownership. "I'll get <u>their</u> coats."

They're is a contraction for <u>they are</u>.

For example:

<u>They're</u> going to the store for ice cream.

Fewer vs. Less

Fewer indicates an actual number.

For example:

There are <u>fewer</u> people here tonight than there were last night.

Less indicates a situation.

For example:

He is <u>less</u> likely to succeed due to his lack of education.

Farther vs. Further

Farther indicates actual distance.

For example:

I can throw the ball much farther than you.

Further is usually not measurable.

For example:

The medication should eliminate any further problems.

Affect vs. Effect

Affect is usually a verb.

For example:

The death of our mother affected us all.

Effect is usually a noun.

For example:

Those diet pills had a terrible effect on his health.

Between vs. Among

Between indicates 2 different people or things.

Bill and George refused to let that old argument get between them

Among is a group.

Let's not fight among ourselves.

Your vs. You're

This is the most common mistake but it's simple to differentiate

Your mean possession.

For example:

I've got your book.

You're is a contraction for *you are*.

For example:

You're my best friend.

It's vs. Its

It's is a contraction for <u>it is</u>.

For example:

I think it's going to rain.

Its indicates ownership.

For example:

That book should be returned to <u>its</u> owner.

Then vs. Than.

Then indicates time:

For example:

I'll see you then.

Than indicates comparison.

For example:

This apple is bigger than the other.

Loose vs lose

Loose mean ill-fitting.

For example:

The chain on my bike came loose

Lose means loss.

For example:

If you keep that up you're going to lose your job.

Elicit vs. Illicit

Elicit means to bring out.

For example:

His speech was meant to elicit a strong response.

Illicit means unlawful.

For example:

Smuggling drugs is an illicit activity.

Emigrate vs. Immigrate

Emigrate means to leave a country.

Immigrate means to enter a country.

To vs. too vs. two.

To means direction. "I'm going <u>to</u> the store."

Too means <u>also</u> or an <u>excessive amount</u>.

For example:

"I'm coming <u>too</u>.

You gave me <u>too</u> much.

Two is a number.

 For example:

"The <u>two</u> of you better hurry up."

Decimate vs. Devastate

Decimate is from the Latin meaning one in ten.

Devastate means to totally destroy.

And finally:

It's <u>used</u> to, not use to.

It's <u>toward</u> not towards.

It's <u>supposed</u> to, not suppose to.

So there you have the basics but don't get too wrapped up in proper word usage. You're not being graded by an English Professor, you're trying to get a book published and enjoyed by your readers. The goal is to be interesting and entertaining. Too much formality can drive readers away.

Section 6-**Avoid common plot contrivances**

There are no REAL rules in writing, that's what makes it art. But writing is also a profession and writers are a dime a dozen. Since your goal is to write a novel good enough to be considered by a mainstream publisher, you'll need to avoid the common mistakes that will likely get you eliminated from consideration.

The first is the, **"AS YOU KNOW, BOB."**

The As You Know, Bob is a plot contrivance the writer uses to pass important information on to the reader. For example: Sam and Bob are doctors having a conversation in some medical facility. They are discussing a patient and what treatment would best suit her condition.

"Nancy's stable now," Dr. Sam said, "but I have concerns."

"Why is that?" Dr. Bob asked.

"Well, as you know, Bob, our patient has a long history of alcoholism and depression. She's been in and out of mental institutions over the last three years. Remember, we were called in two Christmas's ago when, in a drunken stupor, she fell into the pool and almost drowned."

"That's right!" Dr. Bob replied.

In real life people don't trade information they already have. Since Dr. Bob knows the patient's medical history, Dr. Sam wouldn't need to tell him.

Instead, have an outsider bring the reader up to speed. For example:

"Nancy's stable now," Dr. Sam said. "If the tests are negative, I'll release her in the morning."

"I agree," Dr. Bob replied. "I think the danger's past."

"Excuse me, doctors?" a man called out as he approached from the cafeteria.

Both physicians turned. "Can we help you?" Dr. Sam asked.

"You're treating my wife Nancy Smith, correct?" the man asked.

"Yes," Dr. Sam replied.

The man looked around then said, "The family has kept this very hush, hush but my wife is suffering from alcoholism and acute depression. Since that's not on any of her medical records, I thought it important that you know."

Dr. Sam and Dr. Bob nodded. "Thank you for that information," Dr. Sam said. "We'll make note of that when we prescribe her treatment."

And so the reader is informed of Nancy's medical history without the As you know, Bob.

Next is the over used, **"Wait, what was that you said?"**

Here's how it works. The hero is stumped by a seemingly unsolvable problem. No matter how hard he tries, the solution eludes him.

Enter the friend or associate, usually a woman. Concerned, she suggests he take a break and clear his head. He informs her that he can't because there is too much at stake. What follows is some idle chit chat until she says something that, for some reason, the main character NEVER fully hears the first time and so, asks her to repeat it.

For example:

She: "So I told Clara she'd better change her behavior, because job wise, she skating on some very thin ice. When the next round of lay-offs come..."

He: "Wait! What was that you said?"

She (looking puzzled): I told Clara that job wise, she's skating on thin ice and...:

He: "That's it! We'll use dry ice to keep the temperature down!"

With the unsolvable problem now solved, the hero usually kisses the woman and tells her how wonderful she is.

Frankly I can think of 50 movies and a number of books where this is done. You're a creative novelist. Come up with something different.

Next the ever present, **Air duct and Sewer pipe.**

Why is the grate covering every air duct in literature and films never properly sealed? In my experience, every air duct grate I've ever come across was tightly and securely screwed closed. And why are they always just big enough for our protagonists to crawl through?

If I were a super villain, I'd make sure the protagonists were locked in a room where there was no access to the air ducts, because frankly, I wouldn't want them to escape.

Same goes for the sewer pipes. I'd install heavy iron grates every ten feet throughout the pipe to prevent access. Why? Because I'm a super villain, and if I'm smart enough to attempt world domination, I'm probably clever enough not to provide my deadly enemy an escape route.

Again, you're a clever novelist. Come up with something different.

Next up, **"the Disappearing Bad Guy"**

One particularly annoying addition to recent books and films is the disappearing bad guy.

In this scenario, Bad Guy is being chased by Good Guy throughout hell and breakfast. Just as the Good Guy closes in, Bad Guy turns into a blind alley and within the second or two it takes the Good Guy to round the corner, the Bad Guy has magically disappeared!

Or this scenario:

The Good Guy spots the Bad Guy across the street. As a bus zooms by blocking the Good Guys view for about two seconds, the Bad Guy has mysteriously vanished. Unless you created a clever and plausible explanation of why the Bad Guy was able to perform that trick, don't use it. It's cheap, lazy and terribly overused.

Next: **"The Woman's Ultimate Sacrifice"**

Here's how the Woman's ultimate sacrifice plays out. The hero is in big trouble. The antagonist, whose action or inaction may save or kill the hero is sexually attracted to the hero's wife/girlfriend and offers to spare the hero if she sleeps with him. Although she is disgusted by the very thought, she bravely puts her revulsion aside and submits, but only because it is the only way to save her man's life.

This plot contrivance has been used in romance novels throughout time. I'm not telling you not to use it because it continues to remain popular. I only mention it because I didn't want you to think you were the first with that idea.

Superfluous words

One of the most common problem new writers have is using superfluous words and phrases in manuscripts. Many writers make the mistake of thinking they should write the way they talk, because that's the way we have conversations.

Don't do it.

Why? Because in most conversations we drift in and out, we get the gist of what's being said but we're not hanging on every word. Then the conversation goes off on a tangent we're not interested in, so we nod and pretend until it gets to the point where we're considering stepping out into oncoming traffic just to put an end to it.

That's why you shouldn't write the way you talk.

Speech writers write to command attention. It's their job is to make the audience listen intently and hang on every word.

You need to do the same.

Can you spot the superfluous words in the following paragraph?

He had been thinking about going down to the airport to hopefully run into his former girlfriend. After a while he finally decided that he really didn't want to start up a relationship with her again so he turned on the TV instead and watched an old movie on cable.

Word count=49

Here is the same sentence with the superfluous words removed and concise and to-the point words added.

He ~~had been thinking about~~ (considered) going ~~down~~ to the airport to ~~meet up with~~ (see) his former girlfriend, (then) ~~After a while he finally~~ decided that ~~he really didn't want to start up a relationship with her again~~ (would be a mistake) so he ~~turned on the~~ (watched) TV instead. ~~and watched that old movie on cable~~.

Word count=22

The information conveyed is the same, it's done with fewer than half the words and most importantly, it gets to the point. Don't you just hate it when someone wastes your time?

So does your audience!

Remember that when you are editing your manuscript. Start by taking out a word and see if it changes the meaning of the sentence, if not, leave it out. Do the same with the paragraph. If its absence doesn't change anything, out it goes.

When the sentence has been stripped down to the bare essentials THEN, you may add to it, but only use words that make the sentence better, clearer, more to the point, more engaging. Don't bloat your manuscript with unnecessary words and phrases.

An important point to remember is that anyone can take a simple concept and make it seem complex, the sign of a real talent is to take a complex topic and rewrite it so anyone can understand.

Let's talk about the first five pages rule.

As mentioned earlier, the publishing industry is in trouble. There was a time when books were as popular as radio, television and movies. Not anymore. The increasing competition from other sources like the internet, high definition video games, facebook and smartphones are pushing the hard cover book to the back of the line.

There will always be those who love the printed page but even that's being replaced with Kindles and other electronic devices. In today's society things move fast. You have less than 30 seconds to grab a potential customer's attention, 15 if what you're selling doesn't pique their interest.

That's where the first 5 pages rule comes in.

Although there are always exceptions, your manuscript has approximately 5 pages to engage the reader. Gone are the days when you could slowly introduce your characters and their fictional environment over several chapters, or provide an extended backstory so the reader could get a real feel for your novel.

Bottom line. You got 5 pages, thrill me.

That's it folks, 5 pages. So bring your best to the first five because that's your audition. That's where you're expected to dazzle with your vivid imagination and mastery of the art of story-telling.

And to accomplish that goal, here's few things you DON"T do.

Don't start with the weather unless absolutely necessary. It's been done to death.

It was a dark and stormy night!

Don't have your character's use cliché's in dialogue. Statements like, "I heard that! Oh, no she didn't, or Are we all on the same page?" makes you look dull and unimaginative. Create dialogue that's new and thought provoking to catch your reader's attention.

Starting the 'real' story on page 25.

If the real story starts on page 25, then start the book with what's on page 25. Remember tick-tock, tick-tock.

Beginning your book with your protagonist's recollection of past events.

For example:

He remembered his father's advice on the day of his wedding. It was a beautiful summer afternoon and the… Trust me, not popular.

Beginning with a character waking from a dream.

She opened her eyes and looked around. Was she really home and safe in her bed? she wondered. Again, not popular.

Long descriptions of what your character looks like.

For example, opening with 'Her hair was golden and cascaded over her shoulders like a cool mountain stream. Her eyes were... Seriously, a little of that goes a long way, so leave the detailed descriptions for when your reader is already invested in your book.

A long, detailed, descriptive opening.

Remember the clock is ticking. Get your story started now. Events can always be rearranged later during the editing process.

You may consider yourself an artist, and you very well might be, BUT you're not going to get the opportunity to prove it unless you convince an agent or publisher, you can sell books (See marketing tips in the first section). And if you're an unpublished novelist who is convinced your novel needs to be published without any changes or compromises, good luck. You will need it.

The 'KISS' Rule

The KISS rule is the simplest and the most important. KISS stands for **K**eep **I**t **S**imple, **S**tupid. The reasons we write is to convey information, to tell a story, to instruct, to entertain and to enlighten.

You want to share this great thing you have with as many people as possible, so we keep it simple, that way we reach the broadest audience. If it's difficult to understand, most people won't read or recommend it.

One of the most popular writers of the 20th century was Kurt Vonnegut. He had the ability to convey the most complex ideas in the simplest terms. Any nine-year old reading a Vonnegut book could generally understand what he was talking about.

I'm not saying your novels should be written in a manner any child can understand, what I'm saying is that your novels should contain the purest gold of your talent and skill. Not show off your knowledge, the extent of your education or attempt to impress the reader with your mastery of little used words or phrases. In short, keep your ego on a short leash.

Keeping it simple does NOT mean 'dumbing it down. It does not mean replacing eloquent well-crafted sentences with short choppy ones. It doesn't mean replacing a beautiful word with one more easily understood and it doesn't mean cannibalizing great prose into bland text.

What it *does* mean is, that as an author, you have the talent, tools and the responsibility to tell your tale in a way that will engage and entertain your reader regardless of their background or education. Remember, the people who buy and read your novels are your employers. They are spending their hard earned money on a book they expect to be worth every cent.

Make sure it is.

The 'Pick One' Rule

It's human nature to want to give your customers their money's worth. Make them feel as if they are getting a good deal. That's the premise behind the 'baker's dozen,' that little extra to sweeten the exchange.

This is why many writers (myself included) make the mistake of adding an additional word when unnecessary.

For example: The ending of her latest novel left this reader both disturbed and unsettled.

The words 'disturbed' and 'unsettled' generally mean the same thing. If additional description is necessary use a word with a different meaning.

For example: The ending of her latest novel left this reader both disturbed and angry.

So 'Pick One' and go with the word that best describes what you're looking to convey.

Section 7-Polishing your manuscript for submission.

Okay, you've finished your manuscript, your story is complete. What's the next step?

Purchase a notebook, then reread the manuscript and be brutal with your criticism. Write down every word, sentence or idea that is flat out wrong, questionable or simply doesn't feel right and note its location. Because that's what the person you're submitting it to will be doing.

Take an especially cold, hard look at the parts you think are terrific and sparkle with brilliance.

There is an old saying about writers and their first drafts:

They must often kill the things they love.

This is a fact. The reason you must remove these gems is because they <u>are</u> gems, they stand out and interrupt the flow of your story. Before deleting them, write them in a separate notebook for the clever bits you've created but can't use now. Don't worry, they won't go to waste. Somewhere down the road, on some other project, they'll fit perfectly.

Now check your dialogue. Does one character sound like another? Do all your characters sound alike? If so, prepare for some heavy rewriting.

Develop your characters so, with them all in one room, chatting among themselves; your reader can differentiate who the characters are without you having to point them out.

In my Noon series, there is a character named Bali who, because of her bizarre upbringing, speaks like a person from a 19th century romance novel. In my young adult novel, Half Moon Falls there is a girl nicknamed Chatter, because she never stops talking.

Your characters are supposed to be true to life. So give them distinct personalities, and mannerisms that make them stand out as individuals.

Have you constructed a proper setting for each scene? If an important scene has your main characters, say Billy and Bob fighting in an abandoned train yard, you need to give your reader a sense of place, of actually being there as an observer. What do we, as readers, see, hear, smell? What is the landscape, weather? Don't overdo it, just put us there.

<u>Make sure your characters don't 'speechify.'</u> This is a common error. Many times in the heat of the moment, we forget our characters are regular people and saddle them with dialogue that would make Prince Valiant say, "Art thou nuts!?"

This error usually occurs when the main character is about to leave on his or her very dangerous mission.

For example, "Good bye, Sally, I must leave you now for I am needed at the front. I do not know if I shall return but should I not, please remember me in your heart."

Unless this is a story about the days of yore, you'll need to fix this. People don't speak so profoundly anymore.

Here's how that scene should probably read. "Good bye, Sally. I gotta go, they need me at the front. If I don't make it back, please remember all the good times."

What should you watch for in dialogue? People use contractions. The first Good bye Sally didn't have any. It also had, 'for I must' and the word **shall**. When is the last time you used either that phrase or the word 'shall' in a sentence? Seriously, imagine being with friends at a Superbowl party when one of your buddies says to you, "While you're up can you get me a beer?" Would you reply, "I shall. For I am your friend."

Didn't think so.

Another trick is to read your dialogue aloud, or read a scene with a friend. Often, when heard aloud, poor or clunky dialogue stands out.

Is your timeline correct? In the telling of a long and complex tale we often lose sight of what day or time it is. If, on a Tuesday afternoon, Jim goes out for pizza and when he comes back twenty-minutes later, tells his roommate he wants to stay home that evening to watch Monday night football, you have a problem.

Is your location correct? Don't have him drive west from Albany, New York to Burlington, Vermont, because he's not going to get there.

Creating distinct characters

Do not force them to act out of character just so you can move on to the next scene. That's called 'muscling' and will make your story seem forced and stilted and that makes readers uncomfortable.

You have to trust your talent enough to know that wherever the story goes, and however the characters act, it will all work out in the end.

Say you have three friends as the main characters. We'll name them John, Ella, and Terry. In your novel John comes off as edgy and quick tempered, why is that? Perhaps he has quit smoking, or there's family trouble. Ella appears to be a fashionista, maybe she grew up poor and never had good clothes. Terry is a gun-enthusiast, perhaps he had been robbed at gun-point and that experience was life changing.

Do your characters change clothes each day? Can't have Jennifer wearing the red blouse she loves so much, Tuesday, Wednesday and Friday without explanation

Since your characters develop personalities throughout your novel they create their own backstory which makes it possible for your reader to get to know them better and come to enjoy hanging out with them. Better to have the story follow the characters, than to force the characters to follow the story.

From Shakespeare to Harry Potter, if you make your novel a place where readers want to be and your characters people your readers want to be with, they'll keep coming back.

I am often just as amazed at the conclusion of my novels as my readers are and that's what makes it all worthwhile

Remember to take chances. A timid writer has never written anything worth reading

Be Familiar with the Products Your Characters Use.

If your characters are using a specific product, take the time to learn about it because out there, someone is using that product regularly and if you claim it can do something it clearly can't, you lose credibility and likely that reader.

For example don't have four people jump into a Toyota Spyder. (it only seats 2) Don't cock the hammer of a Glock 9 (it doesn't have one) Don't pull down the back seats of a 2013 Hyundai Sonata (they don't fold down). The research will only take a couple of minutes on Google and believe me, it will save you a lot of grief down the road.

Content

People love content. They love to know little interesting facts that other people don't. For example: I thought all lepers colonies were in the Pacific Ocean near the Hawaiian Islands then I discovered there was a leper colony off the coast of the Bronx, in New York City.

It's called Little Brother Island and was used to house people with transmittable diseases like leprosy, smallpox and typhoid until they either recovered or died.

The infamous Typhoid Mary was incarcerated there until her death in 1934. It has since been closed, abandoned and restricted with its shores being patrolled by the Coast Guard.

Well, I couldn't keep that piece of information to myself so I made Little Brother Island a central theme in my novel, *The Resurgence*.

In conclusion, the purpose of writing an unresearched choppy first draft with mixed timelines and speechifying dialogue is to see if you actually had a story to tell. So often people spend so much time preparing a novel that when they finally get to actually writing it, they discover their story peters out midway through, and all that time spent in preparation was wasted.

There are only a few instances where mapping out what you are going to write, works. In memoirs because its history and you want to make sure the timelines sync.

In 'how-to' books, because you want to give clear, step by step directions so those who bought your book can complete their project.

Lastly, in text books and historical novels.

Remember, if you're a fiction writer, make sure you have a complete story before outlining and researching.

Getting your Manuscript Ready for Submission

So let's review. You have completed the first draft of your novel. You have joined a writer group to critique your work and improve your skills, you have removed all extraneous words and phrases, checked your dialogue by saying it aloud to detect speechifying, verified your timelines and locations, created settings that put the reader where the action is and have given your characters discernable personalities. Sound like you're good to go.

Except you're not.

Before submitting your novel to an agent or publisher I cannot stress the importance of having your manuscript PROFESSIONALY EDITED.

For example: Let's say you have built a formula one race car. It's your first one and you're going to test it by driving at Daytona at approximately 200 miles an hour. Don't you think you should have a Master Mechanic give it a thorough inspection before you do?

You know the old saying, "You never get a second chance to make a first impression. That novel is your introduction into the publishing world. Even though you're convinced it is a masterpiece of epic proportions, it is, in actuality, a minefield of grammatical errors, confusing dialogue and plot flaws.

The reason you don't see it is because you wrote it and edited it and have since lost track of what you put in and took out.

You still think Madeline told Fred she put the key under the mat, but you removed that part when you went back and corrected the timeline. Or that Patrick's car accident involved a red Buick.

It does at the beginning but you described it as a red *Pontiac* in the final chapter. Or that Cora is highly allergic to nuts yet she is featured eating an Almond Joy candy bar at the beach with Allen with no ill effects.

These kinds of errors make you look unprofessional, and what's worse, it makes it look like you don't value the agent's or publisher's time. So when I say have it **professionally** edited. I mean hire a professional editor, someone who does it for a living. Not your Aunt Sally the English teacher, or your buddy, Jeff who writes the company newsletter.

If you are serious about being published, put your best foot forward and submit a professionally edited manuscript. Some editors charge a flat rate ($1.50-$2.00) a page for light editing, (more if it requires a complete overhaul). Others charge a per hour rate. Get a break down of their fees before hiring them.

Also take the time to find someone who regularly edits the type of novel you wrote. If they have a Facebook fan page, read the reviews, shop around, ask questions, and get to know them. Ask if they'll edit your first five pages, see if you like what they do with it. If not, try someone else. A good editor is as important to a good writer as a good spouse is to a marriage. Put in the effort and get the right one. You'll never regret it.

A good editor will usually have your manuscript completed within 3 to 5 weeks depending on its size and the amount of editing required. Once you receive it, start making the corrections. Then review the suggestions. Often editors will point out areas where the plot is thin or the dialogue drags.

This is where you must tie up your ego and lock it in the basement.

Writers are sensitive creatures and getting their manuscript returned with red pencil marks covering each and every page can be very disheartening.

But, before your ego convinces you to throw out the edited copy and instead send the original as is…

Don't.

That's it. Don't do it. As your skills improve and your confidence as a novelist strengthens, you will appreciate corrections far more than flattery.

The difference between a professional novelist and an amateur is the professional is always looking for ways to make his/her manuscript better and will accept any hell necessary to achieve that goal. The amateur is starved for praise and flattery and flies into a fury when he or she receives even the slightest constructive criticism.

You want to play with the big kids? Then become one. Put your ego aside and seriously consider each suggestion your editor makes. Remember, he/she has more experience and likely knows what an agent or publisher wants to see. Also of what will sell; and frankly, that is the only thing that matters.

When you hire an experienced book editor you're not only getting someone to sharpen your prose and tighten your plot, you're hiring someone who knows what the public regularly buys and what turns them off.

For example: If your main character is some poor schmoe who takes his misfortune out on his dog, it's going to be damn near impossible to find a publisher or readers.

Why?

Because you can do anything you want to a person, readers shrug it off, but harm a pet? If you let a character abuses a dog or cat in your book, you will make enemies for life! Publicity is one thing, but incurring the wrath of someone who will spend every waking moment trying to destroy your career is foolish and self-destructive.

So if your agent suggests you remove a character or delete a scene and you strongly disagree, then call and ask why. Believe me, editors don't make these suggestions without considerable thought.

There is usually a good reason and you need to listen. Remember if you book succeeds, you both win, if it flops you both lose. I'm not suggesting you make every change your editor suggests, only the ones that make your story better. And you might not be the best judge of that, so go to someone whose opinion you respect, (perhaps someone from your writers group) ask him/her to read both versions, your original and the new one with the suggested changes added and ask which version is better.

One last note and you need to know this.

Even if you do everything right and become a loved and respected author, at some point the critics *will* turn on you. They will dissect your latest novel, piece by piece looking for some fatal flaw they can use to bolster their own career by being the first to label you a hack and a literary light-weight.

If you understand all the flattery, adulation and praise from the media in the beginning of your career is nothing more than a method to sell books and advertising, then you'll also understand that, once you're at the top, the same people who put you there, will attack and tear you to shreds for that very same reason.

Section 8-The Query Letter

Okay, you've made the changes; your manuscript is ready for submission. Do you send it out now?

Nope.

Your next step is the query letter. This is where you knock on the door of the publishing world in the hope that someone will invite you in. This is a very important step, so make sure your query is written with a polite and professional tone.

First, research agents and publishers and find those that handle your genre, (the how and where to find them will be addressed later).

Get the name of the person you want to read it and make sure <u>YOU SPELL THEIR NAME CORRECTLY.</u> Keep it formal, no Hey Jack or Hi Nancy as a salutation. Always Dear Mr. or Ms.

Mention why you chose them (perhaps they represent an author you like or one of their clients referred you.) Give a very quick overview of your book (no more than one or two paragraphs. You can go into details if you are asked to submit a synopsis.) Also, state your qualifications.

For example: You have a MFA or degree in contemporary lit. You write for a newspaper or magazine, you've had articles or short stories published, you have a successful blog (over 10,000) readers, a popular Facebook fan page (over 5000) LIKES etc. Virtually anything that could convince him/her that, should they get your book published, there *will* be an audience for it.

Mention any public speaking experience. They want to know if you can entertain an audience should they send you on a book tour. If you work for a company or belong to an organization that has a newsletter or magazine that would publicize your book, mention it.

What it all boils down to, is you're applying for a job. You want them to hire you to write a book for their company that will make them (and hopefully you) lots of money. The quicker you can convince them of that, the quicker you'll be mailing out your manuscript.

Here's a tip. Don't send queries in August. Most agents and publishers take that month off. Same goes for the time between Thanksgiving and New Year's. This is not to say you stop looking, it means you focus on what actions get results.

Remember this is a business. The big publishing houses and big artist representation companies need to get big sales in order to stay afloat, so they're unlikely to take chances on unproven talent. This is not to say it doesn't happen, it does, but not often. If you're not getting any interest from the bigs try the mid-size and small. One you get in the door you can work your way up.

Note* <u>Never send a query on a fiction novel you haven't finished writing</u>.

Just imagine this scenario. You send a query to an agent with two sample chapters. Two days later you get a call from his office. They want to see the manuscript right away and have already have two publishers interested. Big advance money could be involved, six, maybe seven figures.

You mention that you haven't actually written the book, you only queried to see if the agent would be interested, now that you know they are, you'll get right on it.

You, my friend, have just made an enemy. The only people who can pitch an unwritten fiction story are established writers with a dedicated following and a long association with that agent.

OR

A **non-fiction** writer who has considerable expertise in a particular subject and wants to know if he wrote a book about that particular topic, would the agent be interested.

When you query, make sure you include all your contact information. You name, address, phone number and e-mail address. Also find out if they accept simultaneous submissions.

Seriously, if you want to know if there is a market for your book, check books sales and keywords.

How to copyright your manuscript with the Library of Congress

Please note that copyright methods vary in other countries so you should get legal assistance to find out how it's done outside the U.S.

To begin make a file copy of your manuscript and give it a different title. For example: mybookextracopy.

It is always good to have a second copy (and sometimes a third) of a manuscript you've spent several months, (perhaps several years creating.) just in case something goes wrong

Fortunately, the federal government has stream-lined the copyrighting process, making it easy to use. But because it is a computer program there may be an occasional glitch, but don't worry. If you make a mistake and can't fix it, simply close the program and start again.

The process usually takes no more than 15 minutes.

There are videos on the internet showing exactly how to copyright online with the Library of Congress but the government updates the procedure every few months so any 'How–To' link I place here might be outdated by the time you read this so instead, I'll simply walk you through the basics.

Here's a few things to check before starting. Make sure the version you want to copyright, is the one you're going to upload. Over the course of writing your novel, you may have saved various versions, so be sure you have the right one. Next, check your format. If you skipped the formatting portion of this book you might want to give it a quick review. By using the margins, fonts, sizes and format listed, and by saving it in Microsoft WORD, odds are you won't have any problems. I never have.

Have your credit or debit card ready. At the end of the copyright process you will be taken to a website to pay the $35.00 (US) fee before being allowed to upload your manuscript

Okay, so let's get started. Go to their website at http://www.copyright.gov/ Notice it says dotgov not dotcom and follow the instructions. You will be taken to where you will fill out your personal information. Once completed follow the directions to begin the actual copyright process

When you reach this section, you will be asked to disable your browser's pop-up blocker. Do so, then go to the left and click on Register a New Claim

This is the first part of the copyright form. Click on the arrow on the drop down menu below where it says type of work and click on Literary Work. *Note, before you continue to the next page, write down the Case Number just above the toolbar. This is your reference number. Hold on to it until you received the actual certificate of copyright. Once done, click CONTINUE.

You will be taken to the next part under Title. Click NEW and follow the instructions. Once completed click CONTINUE

On the drop down menu for title type, select Title of Work being registered. In the box below fill in the name of your book. Then go to the top and click on save. You will be returned to the previous section where you click CONTINUE

The next page is **PUBLICATION/SELECTION** Answer the 2 questions and click CONTINUE.

The next section is **AUTHORS**. The advantage here is that the ADD ME button is now available. So instead of filling out the requested info over and over click ADD ME whenever the situation calls for it. Once done click CONTINUE.

NOTE* This section will reappear in case there is more than one author, if you are the only author, and have already clicked the ADD ME button and your name is on the bottom. Click CONTINUE and move on.

Continuing under authors, click the TEXT box and click save. That will take you back then click CONTINUE.

This will take you to the **Claimant** box. Just click on ADD ME and click CONTINUE.

Next up: **Limitation of claim**. This only applies if you are adding to a previous work, if not click CONTINUE.

Next is **Rights and Permissions**. Read the info and if interested click on ADD ME

Then comes **Correspondent.** Just click ADD ME and CONTINUE

Next is **Mail Certificate**. Just click ADD ME and CONTINUE

Then is **SPECIAL HANDLING**. Be Careful, it costs 750 dollars so I suggest you click Continue and move on.

Finally we have **Certification.** Here is where you certify that you are the author(s) and fill in your name. Once completed click CONTINUE.

The last part is **Review**. This is where you check to make sure you filled out everything correctly. Once done, move on to the **PAY** section. Fill out the information and when accepted, go to SUBMIT.

Follow the instructions then click the **BROWSE** button. Go to the file where you have your manuscript (Most likely documents) click on it then **OKAY**.

Follow the prompts and note that uploading may take several minutes.

Once completed, you will be informed that the upload was successful and copyrighted with the Library of Congress. Remember to put you reference number in a safe place until your actual copyright certificate arrives. Once received, put that in a safe place. This is your primary protection against someone stealing your story.

Section 9-Writer's conferences and Writers contracts

A writers conference is a public event where writers, agents and publishers get together to trade information, attend seminars and more importantly, it's a place where writers connect with other writers and make contacts in the publishing field. If you're serious about becoming a writer, start attending them.

I understand you're probably a solitary person. Anyone who can spend their day locked in a room behind a computer with no human contact would likely need to be. But remember those attending these conference are just like you.

These are your people!

It's been my experience that when people with similar interests gather, great things happen. They make friends, establish contacts and get leads.

Another advantage is that established writers, publishers and agents sit on panels and answer questions about the publishing industry. That's why they're there, so don't be shy. You can get valuable insights into your work, perhaps a tip on what agent to query or some advice on how to improve your writing.

But most importantly, by attending you get the opportunity to develop your social skills. This is your training ground for the media frenzy that will occur when your book takes off.

You will learn having a quick and ready answer for the question 'What is your book about?" can be very helpful. You'll learn to walk up to people you've never met and engage them in conversation. And how to convince a total stranger you're a person of exceptional brilliance and talent.

You'll learn to think on your feet.

This is where you can actually convince an agent or publishers to read a portion of your manuscript. Make sure you bring copies of the first two chapters and a brief synopsis. No more than 30 pages total. If you can't engage a reader by page 30, your books needs serious rewriting.

And I'm not suggesting you walk around and hand out copies to every agent you meet. This will make you very unpopular very quickly.

Usually they ask you to forward a copy of your manuscript with a note reminding them that you met at the conference and that they requested it.

But on the odd chance they ask you if you have one available, you don't want to have to say "Sorry, no."

And remember, if you're lucky enough to pique an agent's interest, make sure that manuscript is the latest, best written, professionally edited version you can possibly produce. Do not hand him or her a first draft, or a sketchy synopsis of what you intend to write.

Not many people get the opportunity to grab the gold ring and if, for a scant second that opportunity presents itself to you, be ready!

The same goes for the non-fiction writer. Although you haven't written the book yet, bring a sample chapter and a synopsis of what information the book will contain as well as references to any award or certificate that recognizes you as a specialist in that field.

As stated previously, you are basically applying for a job. So bring out the Sunday-best version of yourself.

And although you might disagree and believe you need to be just who you are, and shouldn't change to mollify other people, let me explain something. The people at these conferences have a lot of experience with writers.

They already know that, as a writer, you're likely difficult, unpopular, opinionated and self-absorbed.

That goes with the territory.

But what they <u>need to know</u> is how long you can act and appear normal.

Because for this relationship to work you'll have to convince the public that you're interesting, funny and an engaging person, one who will show up on time, and in top form for interviews, personal appearances, and for radio and television talk shows.

If you can't, you're going to have a hard time getting one of these professionals to invest in you. And yes, there have been difficult, abrasive and anti-social authors who, despite their unreliability, went on to become wildly successful.

Although those few exceptions did well despite themselves, the overwhelming majority of that personality type died, unpublished, unknown and broke.

Getting back to conferences, there are several types. There are general conferences as well as specialty conferences that focus on one particular type.

If you write sci-fi, you're probably wasting your time attending a Christian writers' conference, same goes for a romance writers attending a fantasy, elves and fairies conference.

Once you find one, read up on the featured speakers. This way should you meet them, you can steer the conversation to something they'll be interested in.

Have Business Cards Made

This way, if you make a connection, you won't have to scribble your name phone number and email address on a cocktail napkin. Just hand them your card. This makes you appear professional and prepared.

If you're ready and willing to attend one, and don't know of any in the area where you live, simply Google 'Writers Conferences' and you'll receive a number of options. Wikipedia has an excellent selection of conferences throughout the country.

Although I don't personally recommend any particular conference or organization, Backspace www.bksp.org in New York City provides some very useful information.

Writers Conferences are author's launching pads. It's the place when, after you've learned all the techniques and mastered the skills in the previous sections, you get to impress them with how good you've become.

Comedian Steve Martin was once asked, "How does a person get famous?" He replied, "Simple, become so good they can't ignore you."

Contracts-both Agent and Publisher.

Okay, you've done it. An agent or publisher has indicated interest in your manuscript and you've sent it off. You're wild with elation and anticipation.

However, while you wait for a reply, meet with a lawyer who specializes in literary agency contracts and book deals and have them explain what they do and what they charge.

There are conflicting stories regarding agent contracts, some are complex, others merely a verbal agreement and a handshake. Horror stories abound but most are legitimate businesses that have been around a long time.

Remember, if you become a best-selling novelist, they'll want to keep you as a client so they're not going to play fast and loose with the rules.

Nevertheless, read up on it. There are several informative articles and guidelines in both of the Guides to Literary Agents and you *should* familiarize yourself with them, however, I would never sign a contract until a lawyer that specializes in agent and book deals looked it over. Lawyer fees are often expensive but there are a lot of tricks that could result in your agent getting far more out of the deal than he/she should.

If an agent or agency shows interest in your script, google them. The more successful the agency, the more articles will be about them. That also goes for disreputable agencies.

See what your fellow novelists are saying about the people you're considering signing with. Are they complaining about how they were treated? Any possible lawsuits on the horizon? Or are they instead signing big-money mega deals for their clients. Believe me, it pays to know, because it's the actions you take now that will likely affect you for the rest of your writing career.

This is also a good time to seriously delve into the business side of book publishing. Since you plan to be part of it for a long time, learn how it works.

There is an old saying. "He who doesn't keep a close eye on his business, soon gains a partner. You may balk and say you became a writer so you wouldn't have to deal with such matters, but there is a lot of money involved and a lot of temptation to skim off the top, so take the time to learn the ins and outs so you don't wind up with a multiple partners.

And trust me, you don't get that money back, it disappears in lawyer's fees and gambling debts and Cayman Island accounts etc.

Also start looking for an accountant or accounting firm that has experience with the publishing industry. If you become successful, you'll want a professional to keep an eye on the books and to keep you aware of what money is coming in and what's going out.

One important note* Never allow anyone to write checks in your name or give them the ability to electronically withdraw money from your business accounts. Pay your own bills online or sign your own checks. You may have to sit down each month and spend a few hours reviewing invoices and writing out payments, but you'll know where every dime goes and won't wake up one morning to discover your business manager has disappeared, all your money is gone, and the IRS is preparing to auction off everything you own.

Next, start searching for a publicist. Although it's going to take at least a year before your book hits the stands, the more leeway time your publicist has to prepare, the better.

And this all may be unnecessary. You might be snapped up by a literary agency with a sterling reputation, be published by a highly respected publishing house with an army of accountants, publicists and editors to tend to your every need.

You might. But what if you aren't? Wouldn't it be a good idea to have a team of professionals at the ready, just in case?

The point is, you've worked so hard at developing your craft so you could make a living as a novelist, why not put in just a little more effort to make sure that when you're no longer in demand, you've a sizeable financial cushion to prevent you from having to deliver pizzas or selling fries.

Before moving on to the next section I want to impress upon you the necessity of not letting the excitement of getting an agent or publishing contract keep you from doing the legwork necessary to ensure everything remains on the up and up. Believe me, the excitement will die down, but signing a contract that rips you off will haunt you for a lifetime.

Section 10-Final edits and book tours ·

When you meet with your publisher, they will likely tell you how much they loved your book, and that you have a great future as a novelist. Then you will be asked to make changes to that book they loved so much, often significant ones and often not for the reasons you'd think.

Many of these publishing houses have partnerships with other industries that sell other products. For example, you may have to remove a section where your character rants about peanut butter. It's funny, touching and one of the highlights of your book, but the company that owns your publisher has a subsidiary that is one of the world's largest peanut butter producers and they're not going to let you bad mouth a product that has steadily increased the corporation's profits over the last 4 years.

Then there are social issues. If your character is on the unpopular side of a touchy social issue, you will likely be asked to rewrite it with the social concerns removed.

You may be asked to add or remove a character, change its nationality, religion, social status and a number of other things they deem some readers might find offensive. In today's hypersensitive society no corporation is going to risk having your novel setting off a national firestorm of protest and a boycott of their many diverse products simply because you commented on a particular issue via your novel.

My personal experience with this issue was when a major university press indicated a strong interest in my second young adult novel Half Moon Falls. So much so they told me they wanted it to be the flagship of the following year's releases.

As I prepared to sign contracts and make plans for another book tour, the requests for changes started coming in. First the last name and nationality of the villainous sea captain had to be changed because it was clearly Korean.

Then I was told **any** foreign sounding name had to be changed so that the university would not be viewed as hostile to foreigners. Then the creatures on the magic charm bracelet were from different mythologies and as such needed to be changed to ones without any mythology at all. Concerns that the man made of mud might be mistakenly viewed as African-American.

This continued until someone on the inside informed me that one person on the faculty had taken control of the project and their rival was determined to kill it.

But it is not all horror stories. Most times the changes do improve the book and more importantly, make it more marketable.

And you need to know this going in.

There will be no contract if the marketing department decides your book is too difficult to sell. So, if you balk at making changes, interest in publishing your book might quickly disappear.

The Book Tour

Depending on the size of the publisher you've signed with, a book tour can be an exciting adventure or a grueling life-sucking experience. If you're fortunate enough to warrant a full blown publicity tour with all the bells and whistles from your publisher, good for you. Once you've reached this pinnacle you don't need any further advice from me. You have booking agents, publicity agents, and personal assistants taking care of these things while you enjoy the adventure of a lifetime. Good-bye and good luck.

As for the rest of you, get ready to buckle down to some long drives, cramped plane flights, unenthusiastic book store managers and customers that shun you as if you stepped in something vile.

Okay, so you didn't sign on with one of the big publishing houses, or the midsize publishing houses. You did manage to sign with a promising up and coming publisher who's had moderate success and whose authors are steadily increasing in popularity. They aren't big enough to book you on Good Morning America or Today or The Daily Show, in fact no national television exposure at all, but they did line up interviews on local news shows, radio programs and have scheduled books signings at the Barnes and Nobles bookstore chain and popular independents.

When my first young adult novel, Frostie the Deadman was published, my publisher booked me at just about every bookstore within a 500 mile radius and on several local TV news shows. I didn't mind, in fact I was enthusiastic. The first leg of my tour was at a Barnes and Noble in Utica, New York. The turnout was fantastic. There were at a least 100 kids who had come to hear me read from my book and get autographs. I was under the impression this was how it was going to be at every stop.

Nope.

I foolishly assumed that because I was a published author, whose book poster featuring me and the cover of my book was in the windows at Waldenbooks, Borders and Barnes and Noble's, people would flock to meet me, buy my book and get an autograph.

Hell, I was somebody.

This is not how it works. If you're an unknown first time author like I was, nobody cares about you or your book and they will purposefully avoid making eye contact for fear you will try to rope them into buying your novel.

So there I sat at my little card table in the center of this giant bookstores, surrounded by copies of my book with people keeping a greater distance from me than they would had I been highly radioactive.

Turns out there had been miscommunication as to who was responsible for publicizing my appearances. The Book Store (It was one of the bigs that is no longer in business) believed the publisher would be handling it, and the publisher thought the book store was handling it. In the end, nobody handled it.

The reality is, these things happen, and more often than you'd think.

Not intentionally, I got along well with my former publisher and would consider working with them again. But to be honest, the real person at fault for this fiasco was me. Yep me. This was my career, my future and I was letting other people handle these details because I was too busy imagining what my life was going to be like once I hit the best seller list and Hollywood called to inquire about movie rights.

Word to the wise.

If someone is not being specifically paid to publicize your personal appearances, and is instead saddled with that job due to their employers financial constraints, their heart in not going to be in it.

Besides, if they accidently forget to contact the local newspaper, television or radio stations, that thankless job might be taken from them and given to someone else.

What do they care if you become a successful novelist, it's no extra money in their pocket. So if your publisher doesn't have someone specifically in place to do that job before you set out, get a list of where you're going, the names of the newspaper, television and radio station managers and call each one to verify the time, date and location of your appearance. Give them your cell phone number so they can notify you of any sudden schedule changes.

Remember this is your career, and the rule here is not to trust your future success to anyone you can't fire or replace.

Another good piece of advice is to be ready for anything and not panic when something unexpected happens. Here's what happened to me during my book tour.

I was booked with two other authors to give a talk and sign autographs for three different age groups. The topic? How to Tell a Scary Story.

The first author was supposed to address the 4 to 7 year olds with his picture book about ghosts, the next author—the 8-11 year old crowd and I was to wrap it up with a read from Frostie the Deadman for the 12-15 year old kids.

I drove for 5 hours to get to this book store and when I arrived I discovered the other 2 authors cancelled and what was worse, when my crowd, the 12-15 year olds saw the younger kids gathering with their mothers in front of the podium, they left.

When I arrived the book store manager was in a panic having seated at least twenty mothers with their 4-7 year olds expecting a show.

That's right, I said 4-7 years old. So obviously I couldn't read from my young adult horror novel and I couldn't leave the store manager in this situation because if I did, you can bet my book would have disappeared from that book store's chain.

Fortunately, I was no stranger to being on stage and had no problem with public speaking as I had been the lead singer in a rock band for many years.

So I took to the podium and winged it. I asked the kids to tell me the things that scared them and with each response took down their names, once done, I made up a story with those same kids in a haunted house, facing all the things that frightened them, except in this *special* haunted house, it was the monsters who were afraid of the kids. I managed to stretch it out to 45 minutes and got rousing applause from the kids and their moms when I wrapped it up.

The manager was so grateful he scheduled a second appearance for me at the end of the following month and heavily publicized it. That day I sold close to 40 copies.

My point is, once you're in the public eye, a career can be made or destroyed in the blink of an eye. You have to learn to think on your feet.

What would you do if, while promoting you vampire and demon book, you discovered the show you're taping is a radical Christian bible show and your interviewer is a fanatic whose questions are becoming increasingly hostile?

Or if you're giving a reading at a bookstore and one of the customers continuously interrupts and argues with you because he doesn't agree with your book's political agenda?

What if midway through a radio interview your host starts bad-mouthing your book hoping you'll lash out and create enough controversy to bolster his ratings?

It happens and you need to be able to handle it.

If you're scheduled to visit a town's bookstore to do a reading and signing, call that bookstore, pretend you're a customer, and ask if they have your book in stock. If the person answering the phone says yeah, they're pretty sure, ask them to check because you don't want to drive all the way there and find it's sold out like it was at that other bookstore you went to.

If they take the time to do this, be polite and thank them. This way the person you spoke to now knows where the book is and can comfortably recommend it because it sold out in that other book store.

Here's another situation.

I was scheduled to give a reading at a big, popular bookstore that had a number of steady customers. I figured I could sell a number of books and create some buzz to get people talking about it. So I went to the store two weeks beforehand and the place was busy. I expected to see my book in the window or a poster advertising my scheduled appearance.

Nada.

So I went searching the aisles of the young adult section, children books, horror and couldn't find it anywhere. So I approached this matronly looking

107

woman behind the counter and asked if they carried *Frostie the Deadman*. Well, she gave me this shocked look, pulled back and with an indignant expression said, "Well, I certainly hope not!"

Although her response nearly caused me to explode, I calmly asked if she were the manager or owner. She replied that she wasn't and I asked if she would be kind enough to get that person for me.

When I met the manager I made no mention of the counter-woman's comment. I simply informed her who I was and asked why the book and promotional materials weren't being displayed. She replied that she hadn't gotten around to it because they were so busy.

How would you have handled it?

I'll tell you what I did. I said, 'I can see how busy you are and if it would help, I'd be glad to put up the promotional materials and load the shelves with my books. This way we can both take advantage of the heavy traffic your store is having.'

And so I did and made a friend who told her employees to recommend my book and to promote my future appearance.

There is an old saying in show business. Be kind to the people you meet on the way up because you'll meet those same people on the way down.

Section 11-Develop the skills necessary to succeed

As mentioned earlier, in order to become a successful novelist you're going to have to develop your people skills. As an artist and writer you may mistakenly think that the only skill you need is a mastery of the written word.

This isn't true. If you've taken the time to research the books presently topping the best seller list, you'll notice that several have a huge fan base but aren't very good. So how did they get published and how did these mediocre books become best sellers?

Simple. The author sold him/herself, marketed heavily and collected positive reviews.

They convinced the buying public via television and radio interviews, public appearances, newspaper and magazine articles and advertisements that their book was the next MUST READ.

A book doesn't have to be phenomenal to become a best seller. As mentioned in the first section of this book, with the right marketing and with an author willing to do anything and go anywhere to push his/her novel, it only has to be okay.

Remember everyone loves a person who entertains them and can make them forget the trials of daily life. In addition, people want to a part of something, want to be included in the latest fad. This is why merchandising is such a big business. How many T-shirts have been sold over the years with some rock band's logo on it, or Harry Potter or Twilight?

Start thinking of ways to make your novel the 'next big thing'.

How to contact literary agents

Literary agents make a lot of enemies.

Why? Because they're dream killers. People mistakenly assume that since they learned HOW to write in grade school, they can simply sit down when the opportunity arises and write a best seller. And indeed people have done just that and their book roared to the top. And when that happens, the media runs with it, giving people the impression it happens all the time.

It doesn't

So if you've decided to write a book without taking the time to learn the craft, or see if there is any interest in the topic; with each submission, purchase a lottery ticket. The odds of you being signed and becoming Powerball's next winner are about the same.

The biggest problem agents have is that writers often don't understand the business. They write a book, have it edited by their wife's sister and then send it to an agent expecting a call in the next few days with the agent telling them they've already lined up several publishers.

While they're imagining what it's going to be like to be rich and famous, days and weeks pass, then months without a word. They start making calls, leave their name and number, but the agent never calls back.

Bastard!

What's ironic, is that writer, who now hates that agent and is bad-mouthing him/her to anyone that will listen, doesn't realize this situation is his or her own fault.

That's right, he's the one to blame, not the agent.

It is not the agent's job to make that person's dreams come true. The agent's only job is to find books that will sell.

That's it. Nothing else.

And until that author recognizes that reality, any submission or query letter sent, will likely be a waste of time.

Want to increase your odds? Well, you've taken the first step by purchasing this book and learning the ropes. The second step is to do research. Find out what books are selling. Who's writing them? Who's publishing them?

Research these successful first time authors and learn how they got published. Find out who their agent is.

Next step, get a copy of either **Jeff Herman's** or **Chuck Sambuchino's Guide to Literary Agents**.

Both are excellent sources that provide the names, email addresses and websites of the most popular and successful agents in the business.

They clearly outline what the agents are looking for, what publishing houses they've sold to and often what authors they represent. They tell you what the agent's percentage is, what they charge for foreign sales and just about everything you need to know.

And get a current edition. The publishing business changes very quickly. What was the accepted manuscript submission policy last year, may no longer apply.

Although both books are well respected and strive to provide only reputable agents and agencies, before you set your sights on a particular agent, check them out on Google because things change.

One last note on this: Few reputable agencies charge a fee to read your novel but this is not to say all agencies that charge a reading fee are disreputable. Just be careful. There are a lot of predators out there looking to scam the inexperienced.

Here are some other things you need to know.

Having an agent greatly increases your odds of getting a contract. They know all the ins and outs of the business and more importantly, who's buying.

Big author representation firms need big sales. If your book takes a fresh look at a popular topic, that's where to start. It gives the agent a built in sales pitch.

For example, vampire stories become popular every ten years or so. As the undead, they disappear from the shelves for a while then come charging back with the next generation.

Mash-ups are currently popular. A mash-up is where you take two popular genres and put them together. For example, the combo of the Wild West and sci-fi gave us Cowboys and Aliens. Vampires and popular people from history gave us Abraham Lincoln, vampire killer.

As mentioned in earlier sections, it is always a good idea to have something to sell when you're selling yourself to an agent. For them to convince a publisher your book will top the best seller list, it is a good idea to have a platform already in place.

And by that I mean develop a following. Each day I publish a new post on my blog. http://zackaryrichards.blogspot.com I don't restrict it to writing tips, because I want to reach as many people as possible. Thousands of people flock to my blog to read my 2 page stories. I write titles that attract readers. For example, some of my more popular posts have been: "I Love Criticism', 'Ahoy, Scumbags!' and 'Sex-talk, Politics and the Hulking Imbecile'. Crazy titles yes, but it piques reader's curiosity and my blog gets another reader. Let people sample your work for free before asking them to buy it.

On my business blog, I go to Google Keywords and find topics in business people are looking to read about. One very popular series was called 'How to Start an Online Business with no Product, No Experience and No Money.

I do the same with Facebook, I attract readers, 'Friends' and LIKES by sharing information, music, art and just about anything they might find interesting.

I also post on Twitter.

I can't stress the importance of having a following. The bigger the following, the more likely your book will be considered for publication.

BECAUSE THE TRUTH IS, NOBODY REALLY KNOWS WHAT IS GOING TO SELL.

So having a ready-made audience will go a long way in convincing agents and publishers you're somebody worth taking on.

Investors only invest in products they are convinced the public wants and when you take a realistic look at it, agents and publishers are just that, investors.

To prove this point, have a look at the Beatles. The most popular rock band in history would probably never have become famous if not for their fan base.

Their ride to the top began with a fan asking Brian Epstein, their future manager about an obscure record they had released called *My Bonnie*.

Intrigued by this girl's obsession he went to see them perform and was blown away by the screaming crowds that packed the club every night.

He signed them and took their tapes to every label in England and was turned down by everyone, with one exception. And the only reason they agreed was because Epstein convinced them the band's huge following would generate sales.

And even after they had monster hits in England, none of the top labels in America would sign them. It wasn't until Ed Sullivan saw them and their legions of screaming fans in England, that he realized they were the next big thing and booked them on his show.

The rest as they say, is history.

I hate to destroy any fantasies or illusions about being a published author but when you get down to it, you are just another person starting your own business, which is writing and selling books.

And like anyone starting a business you're going to have to work your tail off. You've written a book? Great, how long will your editor need to edit it and for you to do the rewrites? When will you advise your list of followers that you have a new book on the way? How many online reviewers have agreed to take a look? Who is doing the video promo for YouTube? When can you deliver the follow up?

Your first television appearance

Unless you have experience being on stage or on television, your first appearance on a TV show is going to be something special, perhaps even terrifying.

Many a normal, well-adjusted person has transformed into a blithering idiot once the cameras started rolling. This doesn't have to happen. Television appearances can be pleasant and enjoyable, once you learn what to expect.

One way to overcome the nervousness of making your first TV appearance is to desensitize yourself about being on camera. Roll play with a few friends or relatives by acting out what will likely happen during those few minutes on air, as many times a possible before your scheduled appearance.

Tape these exercises, then study the tapes. Begin with having your friend announce your name, then walk across the room to the chair opposite your friend, smile and shake his hand, just like you would if being introduced on a talk show.

Then sit in a chair surrounded by spotlights bright enough to prevent you from seeing anything more than a few feet away.

Have your friend keep the questions secret until you begin filming. Then do it just like they do on

TV. Remember to smile and to appear relaxed. Act like you do this all the time. The more relaxed and at ease you appear, the more the audience will connect with you. No one wants to watch somebody cringe, sweat and act like they are being strapped into the electric chair.

As your friend starts the interview, have the other friend with the video camera swoop around you and film you from different angles. This won't actually happen but it will give you some experience in learning how not to stare into the camera, to ignore the peripheries and focus on being calm and keeping the atmosphere light.

Have yet another friend shout out something like "You suck" or make a loud noise, or drop something, anything to distract you and make you lose your train of thought. Again, this is to teach you how to avoid being rattled by something unexpected.

Coming off as relaxed and casual when several million people are watching is a learned skill. The more you do it, the better you become.

Comedian Jerry Seinfeld once told the story of his first Tonight show appearance. He knew it was his big break so he practiced his 5 minute routine for hours at a time, determined to be *so* prepared that, should he fall into a coma the minute he stepped out on stage, he'd still be able to perform his routine exactly as practiced.

You can avoid problems by being so prepared, that should your mind go blank, you'd still be able to answer any question asked by the host.

I always compared being on stage or on TV to be like jumping into a pool without first testing the water. You're in shock the first couple of seconds, but having done it before, you know what to expect and quickly adjust.

If you doing a segment on a news show, there won't be any walk on. When the segment begins you will already be seated and connected to a microphone.

The newscaster will welcome you and get straight down to business. Remember to breathe normally and be conscious of the speed in which you're speaking.

When nervous, people have the tendency to talk too fast. If you do, you might run one word into another and lose your audience.

Another way to prepare, is to record your voice reading aloud for ten minutes. Play it back and see if you're speaking too quickly. Practice until you learn to speak at the same relaxed speed every time you record.

By doing this you'll likely notice your regional accent. And regional accents can be off-putting. Believe me I know.

There are literally thousands of hours of my voice on tape, but in every one, I was singing not speaking. It wasn't until I narrated an audio book that I noticed what a thick New York accent I have.

I rerecorded several of those audio book chapters because of that issue. My accent is still noticeable, but, you should have heard it *before* I made the adjustments.

Once you notice your accent, write down the words that are the most prominent. For me the words: talk, autograph, and government stood out as tawwk, awtagraf and gubmint.

To correct this I changed the spelling on the script to its phonetic pronunciation. Now I tok about ottographs with the gov urn ment.

Where I live in the North Country people leave out the T in words. For example: Kitten is pronounced as Ki-in. Mountain as mao'in and Little as lil. They also throw in an o before i turning Mike into Moike and Ice into Oice. No matter where you're from, you're going to have some kind of accent, and unless it gives you some sort of homespun appeal or makes you stand out in a positive way, try to omit as much of it as possible.

If there is any problem with your teeth, have them fixed before the tour. When you're on TV or in a bookstore talking about your books, you don't want people staring at your mouth wondering why you haven't had that protruding snaggletooth tended to.

Next thing. Get in shape. If you're overweight (and a lot of us are because we spend most of our time sitting behind a computer) go on a diet, start eating right and begin a daily exercise regimen. I'm not talking about becoming buff. Just don't look fat. Buy clothes that make you look sharp and professional.

Next, accumulate entertaining stories. If you make it to the national market, meaning The Daily Show, Charlie Rose, the Colbert Report, and the afternoon talk shows like Ellen, you're going to need several interesting stories, because you can't tell the same one on every show.

If you're working your way up and are booked on the local shows, try your stories there, see how well they go over. The ones that work, sharpen, the ones that fall dead, drop and replace. This way, when you hit the national markets, you'll have a number of good stories that are proven crowd pleasers.

Remember this is show business. Be interesting. Stand out.

I'm not suggesting a rainbow wig and a cape but do something that sticks in people's minds. For example Author Tom Wolfe always wears a white suit (which, by the way is not recommended for television). Truman Capote wore a Panama hat.

Keep in mind they're going to pin a microphone on you, so a turtleneck shirt is probably not a good idea. Busy and complex patterns don't focus well and jeans make you look like a member of the crew.

Sparkly jewelry will flash on camera and remember to turn off your cell phone. Just think how stupid you'll look if you're making your first appearance on the *Tonight Show* and midway through, your cell phone starts ringing.

That will send your creditability right out the window.

As Your Career Takes Off Never Forget The Following:

You're only as good as your last book's sales.

These people are not your friends. You may think so because they are working very hard to establish you as a noted and successful author, but they will drop you without a second thought should your sales drop or you lose your readership. They love you because you make them money. They will stop loving you the minute you no longer do so.

You're out on that publicity tightrope on your own. One misstep and the media wolves will devour you. So if you are asked questions like "Have you ever used a racial slur? Ever spank your child? Ever smack your dog with a newspaper for crapping on the rug? Do what all clever politicians do, answer without addressing the actual question.

Have you ever used a racial slur? You reply, "I am now and have always been an ardent supporter of equal rights. The African-American, Latino and Asian and Native American communities have all made meaningful contributions to our society and we are far better off with them than without them." Then use it as a way to bring the topic back to your book by adding, "In my novels I've always had my characters defend personal and civil liberties because…"

Have you ever spanked your child? Your answer, "My children are the highlight of my life. They have filled it with joy and taught me the importance of family. But when my daughter Sara was a little girl, she would often come to me and ask why I spent so much time writing. I explained that my readers are like family to me and it's important that I spend time with them too and I do that by writing my books and…"

Keep doing this and the media will realize you're no lightweight who can be trapped into saying something that will ignite a self-destructive firestorm. Even so, remember, the media is not your friend and are writing and filming you ONLY because you're newsworthy not because they're fans.

Well friend, that's the basics. You now have all the tools you'll need to submit the best possible manuscript to an agent or publisher. You also know what to do regarding a contract offer, what to expect on a book tour and how to prepare for your television appearance.

One last piece of advice. Write whenever possible. The more material you produce the more interest you will attract and more importantly, the better writer you'll become.

Part 2: Going the Self-Publishing Route

In this section you'll learn:

- Where to get your own ISBN number (most book stores won't carry your book without one.)

- How to properly upload your manuscript to Kindle

- What to write on your disclaimer page.

- How to create your own brand and publish your own books.

- Where to get a professionally designed company logo at a very low cost.

- The secret to acquiring an inexpensive—yet-professional looking book cover that separates your book from the many cheap self-published, vanity press editions already out there.

- Why going the 'Print on Demand' route is a recipe for failure.

- How to get your books into book stores and gift shops.

- The ins and outs of using book printers and how your book can look like those created for major publishing houses.

- How to create a free professional looking book trailer with just 'drag and drop' skills.

- Where to get a website

- What a blog is and how it can help sell your books.

- How to find the booksellers in your area and around the country.

- Where you can purchase marketing materials to promote interest in your books.

- The best books on marketing you can borrow from any library.

- The best websites to promote your novel.

- Where to get your book reviewed and have those reviews posted on Amazon.

Okay, let's dive into the self-publishing process.

Section 12-Getting Started

Being published by a big, well known publishing company and self-publishing have many similarities. The most important, as a self-publisher, is that your novels have the highest quality production, design and presentation.

If you were to line up nine books put out by publishing giants and inserted your book with them, No one should be able to know, in any way, which one is the self-published one.

Your cover must be of the highest artistic quality, the binding professionally constructed, the back cover blurb professionally written, the ISBN code placed correctly, your company logo on the spine and back cover. The inside title properly centered, followed by the disclaimer page, (this applies to physical books). In most cases the opening paragraph of Chapter One is usually approximately one–third of the way down the page.

What's the point of all this?

If you are to be taken seriously as a published author, then your book must reflect that. It must be as good, if not better, than the other professionally made books it shares the shelves with.

When I attend book fairs I note that nearly 2/3rds of the attendees have had their novels created by Print-on-Demand or vanity presses.

This is a waste of time and money unless your book is only being shared with friends and family. Otherwise, if you want to be taken seriously as an author, you're shooting yourself in the foot.

In the first part of this book I said that, as a writer, you need to evaluate your competition for sales. As an author you strive to be unique, to present your own writers' voice and style.

You cannot accomplish this when your novel looks just like every other self-published book on the shelves.

Print-on-demands (PODs) and vanity presses offer templates for your covers, many of them are nice, but they're all alike and other authors are offered the same choices of cover and font. Then they try to rope you in by offering to promote your book by selling it on their website.

There are two problems with this. First, to sell your books at a reasonable price you will need to purchase a lot of them (and I mean a lot!) and frankly, have you ever gone to a POD or vanity press in search for a book to read?

Nobody else does either.

In the end you will be stuck with thousands of copies you can't sell.

"But my book is so good. Everybody who reads it says so!"

Unfortunately, that doesn't matter. If you intend to self-publish and make your novel an international bestseller, you have quite a bit of work ahead.

So let's do this step by step.

First, find out if there is a market for what you wrote. If there isn't don't spend your money on having that book printed. That's money down the drain, instead put your money where it does the most good.

Develop your talent. You may have a lot of it but if you break out of the gate too early, the negative reviews will kill your career before it gets started.

Publish a short story on Kindle 'singles'. Use a pen name and charge $0.99 per copy. Use keywords in the title and once it's up and running, start collecting reviews and use them to promote the story on Facebook and Twitter and Linked-In. Create a buzz.

Rinse and repeat.

Create a webpage for the short stories. Wordpress.com and Blogger.com offer free sites and their website building instructions are simple and easy to navigate.

The problem most new authors have, is they think their story is so good it couldn't possibly be ignored.

But here's the problem.

How do you get people to read it? There are other authors with considerable income who can afford to hire professional book cover designers to create top notch covers, professional book editors to make sure their prose engages and IT people to upload their book or short story to Kindle completely error free.

Plus, they have the money to advertise it.

And you're in direct competition with them.

To compete, you will need to purchase specific software to put you on an equal level. Most of these programs are inexpensive and those that aren't offer an extended free trial period so you can evaluate their value before purchasing.

Note* If you buy any of these programs listed through a link in this e book, I will receive a commission. You will be charged the same price for the program should you chose to buy it directly from the manufacturer, but the writers community usually buys from each other because frankly, we need the money more than they do.

We all know that it takes money to make money, but it's often what that money is spent on, and the advantage that expenditure affords that makes the difference.

Let's go directly to the most important element of your book or short story.

EDITING!

I want you to succeed and if you don't get it professionally edited your book will FAIL!

If you spend any money at all, spend it on that!

So let's start with cover design. Most professional designers charge between $800-$3000 dollars (US) per cover. In most cases it's worth it. These professionals have extensive experience and know what covers sell.

But if you don't have that kind of money, the next best step is to license the use of already created photos and illustrations

Here's how:

There are several licensing organizations that, for a price, allow you to use the specific photo/illustration they have. You then select the one that best represents what you're looking to sell.

Most are used for book and CD covers (there are some exceptions regarding use, so read the licensing agreement for details)

The best known companies are

Istockphoto.com

123rf.com shutterstock.com and http://stockfresh.com/?affiliate=63510 which is what I use because they are the most affordable. You can license a professionally created picture from them for about one to two dollars. The others sell packages for considerably more.

Don't use 'free sites" like Google Images. Many of those images ARE STILL UNDER COPYRIGHT so it would be very counterproductive to get your book well-known by its cover and then have to remove it because the owner of the copyright is threatening to sue.

Then you'll probably need to adjust the image size, add or remove other images, add the title and your name, perhaps a reader review, any awards you have won etc., anything that will entice the customer to give your title a serious look. The best way to do this is to purchase Photoshop Elements.

To be fair there are other ways to do this. For example there is a free program called **gimp.org**. It's a satisfactory program similar to Photoshop Elements but many find the learning curve excessive and the program not as reliable. Plus Photoshop has step by step tutorials so you can learn to use it quickly. You can get it for a onetime payment of just under $70.00

And there is Fiverr.com where you can hire someone to do the work for you for usually between $5-15 dollars. But here's the problem, those who are really talented don't remain on fiverr for long. Once they establish themselves they move on the greener pastures. For example, I hired a highly recommended cover designer on fiverr.com to do the cover for this book for 15 dollars. It was obvious that what I received had been outsourced to a less talented designer and one who clearly hadn't created the stunning covers shown in the original designer's portfolio, so I threw it out.

Such is the price of an education.

Next you will need a **<u>disclaimer page</u>**. This is where you state that you have permission to use the lyrics of a particular song. (Not easy to obtain if you're an unknown, so avoid song lyrics and other copyrighted material until your sales are big enough so that your use of their copyrighted material benefits them as well.)

It is also the place where you state that the people, places and things mentioned in the book are fictitious and any similarity to any person living or dead is coincidental. You can copy the disclaimer page from just about any published novel; just make sure you change it enough so that the disclaimer fits your book.

The resource material credits are usually placed in the back and lately the disclaimers in fiction e books are being placed at the end too. Amazon Kindle permits readers to sample the first few chapters and readers become annoyed when they have to slog through page after page of disclaimers, author's notes, dedications and so on. (Remember the first 5 pages rule?)

Okay so you've finished the short story experiment and are ready to place your novel on Kindle. It's been properly edited, the disclaimer is in place and you've purchased or created an eye catching cover.

Now is the time to request reviews.

If you've followed the suggestions made in this book, you've probably made a few friends from your writers group, from Facebook and Twitter and from subscribers to your blog.

These are the people you contact and ask if they will review your novel. If they say yes, email them a PDF or Word copy and hope for the best.

If you're involved with other writers and they are agreeing to review your book, it will likely only take them a few days to finish it so you can go right ahead and upload your novel to Kindle.

Section 13-How to Upload your Novel to Amazon Kindle

We've all gone through it. Uploaded our novels to Amazon Kindle only to see wrong spacing, wrong fonts, no spacing, no chapter separations and the final product looking nothing like the manuscript you uploaded on the Kindle preview. Well I finally got a handle on it and am going to show you how it's done.

Okay, let's start with the basics. First you'll need to put your manuscript on Microsoft WORD. I'm sure it can be uploaded to Kindle from Apple or Corel programs but I don't have those programs so I can't help you if your work isn't on WORD.

First, create a copy of your manuscript and save it under another name, like MYBOOKCOPY for example. **Then close out the original manuscript.** You should have it on disk or flash drive in case your hard drive fails, (We will use the copy should you run into problems with reformatting)

Most likely you have a standard double-spaced manuscript on 8"x11" paper with 1 ½ inch margins. First let's simplify the manuscript so it can be better copy-edited. I've found changing the manuscript size to 5.5" width X 8.5" length (this is trade book size) to have the least problems.

So on your toolbar, click on P**age Layout**, then click on **size**. Then scroll down to '**more paper sizes**' and click on that. Then replace the width with 5.5" and the height with 8.5" then click on **OKAY**

Then click on **Margins**. Scroll to the bottom and click on **custom margins**. Then at **Top:** set it at 1 inch **Bottom:** set it at 1 inch. **Left:** 0.7 **Right** 0.7 then click on **OKAY**

At this point your manuscript should look similar to a paperback novel. Now click on **HOME** on the toolbar, go to the far right and click on **Select**, then **Select All**. That should highlight you entire text in blue. Once that happens, go to the center of the toolbar where the **Paragraph** section is. Click on that tiny box on the bottom right with the arrow inside it.

That will bring up another box. This is how I format my novels so they look like any novel you pick up in a store. If you are writing some tech manual with blocks and columns you may have to play around with this to get what you want (another reason why we always work with a copy)

Okay so, under the **Alignment** dropdown, click on **Justified.** The go down to **Special** and click on **First Line,** then under **BY** −This is where you choose the indentation amount of every first paragraph in your book. Default is 5 but I have found that to be too much when read on a Kindle so

I use 3. Then down to **Line Spacing.** From the dropdown, click on **Single.** Then click on **OK.**

Next, make sure at the end of every chapter you go to **INSERT** on the **HOME** toolbar and click on **Page Break** following the <u>end of the last paragraph of each chapter</u>. This will keep your chapters separated from each other. Also make sure you do it following the title page, the declaration page, and any other page where you don't want the text connected to the text of the following page.

Here where the fun begins. Make sure you are on the **HOME** toolbar and on the Paragraph section used earlier. There you will see a box that looks like a backwards **P** Click on that box. You will notice there are now those backward P at the end of every paragraph. If you see a line of dots before a word, with the exception of the ones surrounding PAGE BREAK........Delete them and any arrow you see. The dots and arrows are indicators of where the text doesn't match the format you've established, and will screw up your text when uploaded.

Here is another important issue. If you want to create spaces between--say your heading chapter and the first sentence, go to **Page Layout** on the toolbar, click on **Breaks** then on the dropdown menu scroll down to **Continuous** and click on that for each space you wish to create.

For example: After the word Chapter One you hit **ENTER** on your keyboard then go to Page layout-then Continuous and click on that. This will also need to be done to create a space between your jump cuts (this is where you put in a space to jump to another character or to denote time has passed.) otherwise each paragraph will be directly below regardless of the spaces you inserted in your original text.

When you are sure everything is the way you want it, click on the backward P again to turn it off. The click on **SAVE**

The next step is to download a mobipocket creator. This is usually free, simple to use and necessary if you want your manuscript to come out looking the way you want it to. Here's the link:

http://www.mobipocket.com/en/downloadsoft /productdetailscreator.asp

After downloading, click on the mobipocket icon. Then under **Import from an existing file,** click on **MS Word document.** At the **choose a file box** click on **browse** and go to your manuscript, click on it (remember to use the copy NOT the original) and mobipocket will import the document.

Then it will convert it to HTML and place it in your **Publications** files. Then at the top of the mobipocket toolbar click on **Build**. This will open another box, click on BUILD and that will complete the process.

Now you are ready to upload your manuscript to Kindle.

Just a note* If you want the 70% commission price your book between $2.99-$9.99 otherwise you'll receive the 35%.

One other note* You will be asked if you want DRM to prevent it from being downloaded from a non-Kindle device. With the number of the type of e readers continuously growing you might not want to lock yourself in with that. Still it's your choice

Now this is very important. When you reach the part on Kindle where you upload your manuscript, **_REMEMBER_** you will find the properly formatted document in **Publications** so don't use the one in **Documents.** If you upload the one from **Documents** you will have wasted your time and it will come out unformatted. Fortunately you can reload it if your first attempt somehow goes wrong

Now that it's done, take the time to review your book in the Kindle Preview to make sure it turned out the way you wanted, but don't be overly picky or you'll drive yourself nuts. There may be some small errors here and there but unless it's really troublesome or screws up the story you're better off leaving it alone.

For example in my book DIVORCE-The Middle-Aged Man's Survival Guide http://amzn.to/ZMvhqx there is a sentence that should be indented. It is at the beginning of a chapter and it annoyed the hell out of me but no matter how many times I went back and tried to fix it, it did not indent. So I learned to live with it. One last note, if this helped you successfully upload your manuscript to Kindle please sample one of our books at http://www.aripublishing.com We do good work and we're sure you'll find something you'll enjoy.

Okay, your book is now on Kindle. Now the time has come to get the word out. Join such sites as www.goodreads.com www.redroom.com and www.authormarketingclub.com

I suggest you use Kindle's KDP Select program to promote your book for free for 2 days. You have the option for 5 days but offering it for free for more than 2 at one time cheapens its value. Remember you are using this to build readership. So I suggest 2 days at first, another 2 days some weeks later and then 1 day several weeks after that.

Studies have repeatedly shown that authors that do 1 or 2 day free promotions acquire readers faster and increase their fan base and sales at a greater level than those who don't.

Once you start selling books you're going to need to create a list.

Here's why:

As an Indie publisher you don't have the same access to a large readership base that commercial publishing houses do. But you can make use of the one you have by having your readers subscribe to your newsletter.

A newsletter keeps your fans up to date on what's next on your creative agenda and when your new books will be released. You can also connect with them by offering— to your subscribers only— parts and storylines that were omitted from your final version of their favorite novels. Doing this shows you appreciate those who buy your books and gives them a feeling of being an insider.

To do this you will need an auto responder. An auto responder is a company that collects your subscribers' names and email addresses and manages the amount of times your readers are contacted. It also provides them with the ability to 'Unsubscribe'

The 'unsubscribe' option is your friend. It lets your subscribers know that they are not trapped into any spam type deal and that should they decided they no longer want to hear from you, they can opt-out just as easily as they opted in. It's also an early warning system to alert you when you are losing your audience or if what you're writing isn't meeting with their approval.

We all know you can't please everyone but you should make a special effort to please those who buy your books. Because without them you'll likely be back behind the counter asking people if they, 'Want fries with that?'

The most popular auto responder and the one that serves the most customers is aWeber.com Here's the link: http://aweber.com/?421597

They charge only $1.00 for the first month then $19.95 each month after that. The bigger your list, the bigger your sales and until you become a national bestselling author, your list is your stepping stone to publishing success.

Becoming a Publisher of Physical Novels

To be honest I don't see much of a future for physical novels. They generate the same problems for small indie publishers as they do for the large commercial book publishers.

And that is, no matter how you look at it, in the end, they'll cost you a lot of money. There are exceptions. Amazon's 'Createspace' is relatively inexpensive but like other POD's their covers are templates and their fonts ordinary. They do make it possible for you to upload your own cover BUT it will likely take a number of attempts before you get it right. This is because the image is set by computer, so if you don't angle it exactly right your printed book cover may come up looking amateurish and poorly designed.

Having Photoshop Elements can help a great deal with this. It gives you the ability to reset the resolution to the required 300. The lower the resolution the less clear your cover will be and your back cover blurb will likely be blurred.

Unlike Kindle books, which don't require an ISBN #, physical books do. An ISBN # is that bar code with the numbers on the back of each novel. They are necessary because almost all booksellers require them. If you want to your book sold in stores like Barnes and Noble you'd better get one.

Createspace provides you with a ISBN number but the ownership of that ISBN belongs to Amazon so should you want to go with a different publisher, you would have to get a new ISBN # and a new book jacket before rereleasing the book. In addition, many bookstores refuse to carry Createspace books because of their affiliation with Amazon.

You can however, purchase an ISBN number from Createspace if you self-publish but to do so you must have an account with Bowker.com. I've had an account with Bowker for years going back to the time when you could purchase an ISBN # for $25 dollars. The present cost is $125.00 per ISBN, so you need to take that cost into account when you consider self-publishing a physical book.

My personal affiliation with Amazon has been great. I have always found them professional and easy to work with. But I don't want them as my publisher. I believe that if you're going to self-publish, then self-publish by owning all the rights. This way you can walk whenever you decide to.

Section 14-Setting up your Indie Publishing Company

The place to purchase your own ISBN# is a site called www.Bowker.com

They have been authorized to sell and distribute ISBN number barcodes. You can buy a single ISBN # for $125.00 (US) on their site

They will download the information and barcode to you. Keep it on file as you will have to forward it to your book printer when your book is ready.

But before you decide on physically publishing a book, here are some things you should know.

1) The fastest route to bankruptcy is to publish a mass market paperback book.

Here's why:

A mass market book are those 4 x 6 ¾'' paperbacks we see on the shelves at bookstores and places like Wal-Mart and Target.

These books are usually outsourced by the original hardcover publisher to a company that produces the paperback by having it printed on giant sheets that can make copies quickly and inexpensively.

You don't want to get involved in this because it costs *a lot* of money to set up. A lot of ink and paper is wasted getting the process started AND most importantly, the mass market paperback is almost always a former best-selling hardcover.

Another drawback of going the mass market paperback route is that it's too expensive to return the physical book to the publisher for a refund of the books that didn't sell. So they tear off the cover and send that back instead.

Bad case scenario: You pay thousands to get your book made into a mass market paperback. You get a distributer and pay them to get it into all the big box stores and book seller chains.

It doesn't sell!

The covers come back like a swarm of locust eating up your money.

But everybody liked the book!

True but *that is no guarantee it will sell!*

One of the facts of the entertainment business is that every so often a terrible movie will do terrific business, a lousy TV show will go straight to number #1 and a poorly written novel will become a cult favorite and make the author millions.

And for each and every one of those flukes, there is an equal and opposite amount of great movies that no one will see. Great TV shows that don't last one season. And classic books that never find an audience.

That's a sad fact but a true one which is why it's so important to learn marketing. Knowing how to get your book into reader's hands may be the only thing that prevents your fledging publishing company from going under.

Who to choose to print your book for publication

Go to Google and type in book printers. Avoid all the vanity and POD companies. Find a book printer that specializes in printing for small indie publishers. Better yet go on Facebook and ask fellow indie authors who they used and would they recommend them. Review their titles and see if they're professional quality. Check Facebook and Google for comment on the quality of their work.

Do your homework. It took me several weeks to finally decide what company Ari Publishing would use. I researched American companies, Canadian companies, Southeast Asian companies and Chinese companies.

After comparing prices and services we decided on an American printer in Florida. They provided a wide range of services, at reasonable prices but since we already had a finished product, we were able to get a substantial number of books printed at a reasonable price.

Their submission system was easy to use, their customer service got right back to us and the finished product was made to the exact specifications I gave them. Ari Publishing's first release was as good, and in some cases better, than books created by some of the top commercial publishers.

Here is the MOST IMPORTANT thing to do BEFORE having your book printed.

Find out what stores are going to sell it!

Go to www.local.com then type in 'book sellers.' in the 'Search Box.' Then type in the name of your nearest major city. Enter that location and you will receive a listing of booksellers in the area of that city.

Next step, take day trip, go to these stores and see the kind of books they sell. If your genre fits in, talk to the owner, tell him if he orders say 7-10 books you'll do a personal book signing at his store.

Explain that you know how to promote it well enough to ensure a sellout of the books he orders. (Do this by contacting those on your list in the area, do a Facebook ad and set it to run only in that particular area and only to Facebook members that have 'reading books' on their personal likes page. Also run an ad on www.craigslist.com and on www.USfreeads.com and write an article and submit it to www.goarticles.com but only in that select area.

Make phone calls to local radio and TV stations, see if they'll interview you as a special interest story. (Local author making personal book signing appearance in town (date and time) and if they agree, practice those tips I gave you earlier so you will be fully prepared and professional.

Remember if you are an entertaining and engaging guest, you'll have no trouble getting another booking for your next novel.

Then a week before the book signing, have your printer create a poster featuring a picture of you and your book. Pepper it with a few very positive reviews. Then place it in the window of the store where you're doing the signing.

Remember you're building a business. Be professional and keep in mind, these people are your future contacts. Let them know that you're willing to do what you can to help their business succeed as well.

So you want your book in Barnes and Noble

It's not as hard to accomplish as you think. They have a webpage explaining the process. Here's the Link:
http://www.barnesandnoble.com/help/cds2.asp?PID=8148

Just remember, before you make your way into the bookstores where authors like King and Grisham and Rowling are sold, have a plan to ensure your books get sold quickly.

And if you're losing heart because you don't have the personality to talk to store owners and books store managers, keep in mind there are companies that specialize in doing those things for you. Once again go to Google and type in publicists, book marketers, press releases etc.

Create an Audio book

The publishing business is changing rapidly and as an indie publisher you can move quicker than big commercial houses to get your book in the hands of the public.

One of the fastest ways to do that is to create an audio book. This book is presently available as an audio book.

Audio books are becoming big, very big. Radio is being replaced by audio books during drive time commutes. They are outselling hardcover novels and will likely soon overtake mass market paperbacks.

I've created one. You can too. Here's where to start: www.acx.com

First, although Audible.com is an Amazon company, the rules are quite different than those for uploading to Kindle.

If you want to turn your already popular novel into an audio book you can and Audible won't charge you, (there is a royalty deal like Kindle regarding sales however.) But there are certain skills you'll need to acquire before venturing into that realm, because you only get two tries to get it right.

That means the narration must be clear, at a normal pace and easily understood. In addition there are no pops, crackles or car horns in the background.)

If it's not professional quality by the second try, you will likely be banned from further submissions.

Also, they don't like self-published books. But if you have regular books on Amazon or e books on Kindle that have positive reviews, you probably won't have any trouble.

Second reason is all audio books must go through their quality control process before being released for sale, (the process takes from 3 to 5 weeks on average.) So if you submit before getting a good handle on what you're doing, you could damage your rep as a skilled and talented writer.

They give you several options on how to have your book recorded. The most preferable is having a professional narrator do it. They have a number of pros to choose from and you may review their work before deciding which one is right for you. The narrator will have to be paid so that's something you will have to work out with them. But one distinct advantage is that the audio version of your book probably <u>won't be rejected</u> because these people have done it before and know what is required.

Another option is to narrate it yourself.

This is what I did. But I had an advantage, having been in a recording studio for the better part of my life, I know how it's done. And if you don't have any experience recording, you're going to have a bit of a learning curve.

Here's another important point. <u>Before you do anything,</u> go to the library and check out audio books similar to yours. Different genres have different lead-ins. 'How-to' books are generally cut and dried, meaning the narrator reads it exactly as written. Fiction generally has music snippets at the end of each chapter. So get one (or several) audio books and listen to see how it's done.

The next thing you are going to need is a recording program. If you have a recent version of Windows it likely contains Windows Movie Maker which has a basic recording program or Quick Time if you have a mac. I suggest you use these to create the 'first draft' of your audio book. It'll give you a chance to get your feet wet and not worry about screwing up because it's only practice.

But once you get serious, it's time to download a professional studio program. Keep in mind you don't have to go all out price wise, those high end programs are for musical groups that are recording CDs that require a number of tracks and editing software. You don't. At best you'll be using only 2 tracks and once you get the swing of things by watching the tutorials you'll find it really isn't all that difficult.

Shop around and pick the one you feel comfortable with. I chose NCH software because they let you test drive the program free for a few weeks to see if you like it. http://www.nch.com.au/wavepad/index.html?ref =4068062

I found it easy to navigate and had no problem converting the finished product to their specs. I would suggest you also give a look at Apple's recording software (I haven't used it so I have no idea of how good it is) only because you have to use Apple's iTunes program to convert and upload to Audible.

So there you have the basics. You next step is to go to https://www.acx.com/help/how-it-works/200484210 and ***READ THE ENTIRE THING ALL THE WAY TO THE BOTTOM.*** (And take notes along the way.) There are many useful tips that will save you re-recording time if you follow them. One last thing you need to know.

Record all chapters separately!

That's how you're going to upload them and if you record the whole book on a single track, you're going to have to do the whole thing over!

One last important note.

It will probably take you a few weeks to record your novel should you choose to do it yourself. So have you given any consideration to how you're going to market the audio book when it's done?

Marketing is the MOST important part of the creative process. Because without it, no one will know about that wonderful thing you brought in existence. In fact, marketing is so important Bill Gates paid The Rolling Stones **11 MILLION DOLLARS** for the right to use their song 'Start Me Up' to launch Windows 95.

As mentioned throughout this book, in order to sell your book you have to find a way to bring it to peoples' attention.

This brings us back to Google keywords tools. But there is a problem. Google will provide the most often used keywords for any topic but too often, that first Google page is loaded with professional companies with countless backlinks.

So even with the top ranking keywords, it's likely your book's website will be buried on Google page 75 which nobody looks at.

The Key to sales are keywords or keyword phrases that will place your book site on Google's front page

So we bring in the big guns. As I said in the beginning of this e book there are some products you will need in order to get your books out before the public. As you have seen many are free and the one's that aren't have a free trial period.

More than enough time to decide whether these product will increase your book sales.

The best software for marketing is called Market Samurai. This product has the most comprehensive tutorial program I have ever seen in an instructional program.

By watching the videos, you receive a clear and concise understanding of marketing and the best methods to get any product out before the buying public. The program immediately addresses the problems you will encounter promoting your book and how to solve them.

And in addition, their software program **_automatically_** sifts through and eliminates nonproductive keywords, and highlights the competition regarding each keyword selected so you can rig your keywords to market to the highest number of people with the lowest amount of competition.

In a sense their program makes it possible for you to be the 'opening act' for a major performer. By using specific and long tail keywords, their program show you how to get your book on the first page of several Google searches.

As I said you get a free trial so download it and give it a test drive. Here's the Link: http://marketsamurai.com

Section 15-Make a Book Trailer Video

As mentioned earlier there are video creating software programs loaded into most computers. Apple has *Quick Time* and Windows has *Windows Movie Maker.*

Both programs are adequate but not good enough to sell your book. If you're going to create a video book trailer, you'll want to make sure it is as good as any professional video promoting a movie or fall premier TV show.

Don't forget, your goal is to be as good as the commercial publishing houses so have a look at the book trailers for their best-selling books in your genre and figure out what made them so popular.

Then begin your career as a video film maker. You can see the video I made for my novel The Resurgence here: http://youtu.be/vn0bliErdPc

Here is exactly how I created that video. Believe me, I never studied video editing, or computer programming. I simply purchased the things I needed and put it all together.

The program I used is from NCH software and is called Videopad Video Editor. http://www.nchsoftware.com/videopad/index.html?ref=4068062 Then I went to www.istockphoto.com video section and typed in keywords like mathematical formulas, scientific theories, revolution, urban warfare, riot, sinister characters, then to the music section and typed in suspense music, danger music etc.

I spent a day or so sorting through videos, illustrations, photos, and music then selected and downloaded the ones I would feature on my video.

You might think that this is something beyond your abilities but it's not. You're a writer, so you're already pretty clever. After you download Videopad, watch the tutorials. They are straightforward and because the system uses a point and click and a drop and drag system, creating a better than average video isn't difficult at all.

Here's what I did.

I purchased and downloaded the video with the floating mathematical formulas to show Noon is highly intelligent, and drop and dragged it to the Videopad editor's video section. Then followed it with the video of the tanks and warfare, then wrapped it up with the sinister picture of a man in silhouette holding a gun gangland style.

Next step, using the subtitle icon on the toolbar I typed in the e book blurb to create interest and to tell our story so far.

Then I took the music I purchased, downloaded and drop and dragged it to the audio track and followed that with the sound of a siren.

At the end I uploaded a photo of my book cover (which I also created myself using an istockphoto illustration and the Photoshop Elements program mentioned earlier in this e book.

With the finished product completed, I uploaded it to YouTube, (Note* Videopad Editor has an automatic upload to YouTube program installed in the software so it's all done for you.

Use Marketing Samurai to get the best keyword tags for your video with the least competition and you will drive consistent traffic to your book. Link it to your e book and audio book and you will have created a triple threat.

Logos and Video Presentations

As an Independent book publisher you're going to need a logo for your company. You can see the logo I designed at the Ari Publishing website

http://aripublishing.com

It looks very professional, but it had humble beginnings. You can watch the how we started Ari

Publishing video here and see what the original logo I designed looked like.
http://youtu.be/GLpDHYX7gzo

The logo on the top right of the Ari main page is the one we use for our publishing imprint. But how did it go from that simple design to the multicolored logo we use today?

www.fiverr.com There are a lot of talented people out there looking to get their work in front of the public and are willing to sell their considerable talents at an affordable price to create their own brand.

I searched fiverr for graphics and designs and clicked on logos. I forwarded my original design and asked him to give it more volume and color. I was very happy with the results.

Another purchase from fiverr that I was very happy with was the video lead in we use to introduce our products. I wanted something that would leap out at the customer and make Ari Publishing a name a person wouldn't soon forget. Here's the YouTube link:

http://youtu.be/Nszhu5VbP7Y

The next produce I wanted was a commercial to introduce people to Ari Publishing so I went to Fiverr and had this gentlemen do the commercial I wrote. Here's the Link:

http://youtu.be/khsvCYQCm8M

I used a woman from Fiverr to promote a video tutorial on How to Get Your Book Published. Here's the Link:

http://youtu.be/OshCWa-JK4I

There are a number of ways you can promote your books and get them into the hands of readers. But you have to be clever and determined.

And here is something else you'll need to understand and it's very important. Book publishing, like any entertainment discipline can be very frustrating. You can spend enormous amounts of time working on a project only to watch it mysteriously fall on its face. Write a book that everyone raves about yet for some reason, nobody buys it.

It's a fickle industry. However, once you manage to secure an audience through your auto responder list and you continuously provide quality content, they'll stick with you through thick and thin.

I read about the making of the movie Jaws, Spielberg's first big project and one that would either make or break his career. The shoot had serious problems from the outset. Nothing was working out. The weather was lousy, the water too cold and choppy. The shark was scheduled to be seen in the early portion of the movie yet, there was so much trouble getting the mechanical shark to work, they had to keep rewriting the scenes so you saw the effects of the Great White but never actually saw it.

Yet day after day Spielberg just muscled his way through it and kept finding ways to overcome the numerous problems.

The result was a colossal hit and to this day Jaws is considered one of the best films ever made so, when you get frustrated and run into problem after problem just keep muscling through them. If nothing else you will acquire a number of amazing skills.

Create a blog and an Amazon Author's page

Creating a blog is very important when it comes to introducing yourself to the world as an author. The main places to create a blog is http://www.wordpress.com and http://blogger.com I have found it's easier to set up a blogger account than WordPress but WordPress is more commonly used and has considerably more apps and links. Give both a look and start setting up.

Check out other people's blogs to see how they are done. Mine is
http://zackaryrichards.blogspot.com

To build an audience quickly you must post frequently. If a certain post generates a lot of traffic, promote the hell out of it and leave it up for a few days until the traffic slows down.

Always reply to comments. Be personal and professional. And expect to get jerks. The more popular your blog becomes the likelier trolls will start spamming your page. Ignore them and see if they go away, if not report them.

Place a link to your blog on Facebook, Twitter and Linked-in.

Most importantly, set up a Facebook business page to promote your books Here's a *'How-To'* link: http://www.socialmediaexaminer.com/how-to-set-up-a-facebook-page-for-business

Another way to generate more traffic to your site is to use your Market Samurai to find high traffic and low competition keywords on the topic you've written about and enter them into the tag(s) section of your blog posts.

As mentioned earlier, create a newsletter and link it to your Aweber auto responder http://aweber.com/?421597 This way you'll be able to develop a relationship with your readers.

Another way to get known is to write articles on http://ezine.com E-zine has a strong following and intelligent readership. This is a great way to make contacts with others in publishing.

Join writing forums in Linked-in, which is another great place to make contacts and learn about writing.

And finally, as I've said over and over again, knowing how to market your book is vital to your success as a novelist and a publisher. The King of book marketing gurus is John Kremer. His link http://www.bookmarket.com has literary hundreds of useful tips to get your book noticed and his book 1001 Ways to Market Your Books is the industry bible. It's available in any library but once you start reading it you'll probably buy it. It's that good.

Summary

My friends, as writers you no doubt bristled at many of the suggestions I've made, especially the ones that stomped on your belief that your first novel would be viewed as a work of genius by literary agents and publishers. That published novelists make millions of dollars and never concern themselves with money matters and that book publishing is a profession more interested in providing the world with great literature than generating huge profits.

My apologies.

So ask yourself, knowing what you know now and realizing what you're probably going to have to do to make a living as a writer, is it still something you want?

Unfortunately, book publishing is portrayed in almost mythical terms. We read interviews with successful authors who apparently spend all their free time delving into the meaning of life, while traveling the world for inspiration.

Does that happen in reality? Sure it does but only for a select few. Do you know who else spends their free time delving into the meaning of life and traveling the world?

Lottery winners.

A good friend of mine is a businessman who has made millions over the years and continues to do so. We discuss what is going on in our lives and he used to chastise me for not spending every waking moment promoting my books.

I'd explain that I'm not that type. I don't like ballyhooing my work, and don't like trying to convince people to read them. Deep down I'm a writer, not a salesman.

I remember that he eyed me for a moment then said I was doing a disservice to the very people who **would** read my books and enjoy them. He said that after our first discussion and my mentioning that I was a writer, he looked me up with the intension of buying one of my books and reading it.

"Do you have any idea how hard it was to find you on line?" he later asked. "I spent nearly fifteen minutes at my computer, trying to track you down so I could buy your book. For one thing," he said, "you spell your first name with a K when most people spell Zachary with an H. You have no keywords to drive traffic to your website, no OTO sales, no special events and your blog hasn't been updated in weeks.

Sadly, he was right. I spent ALL my time on writing, figuring that sooner or later, one of my books would create a buzz and would subsequently rocket up the best seller list. I believed it was only a matter of time. Each book I wrote received great reviews, they would sell well for a period then drop off.

Forgotten.

So I took my friends advice to heart. I stopped writing books and focused on getting readers. I began blogging every day.

I joined an affiliate marketing company and started studying how to get a product out before the buying public. I took advantage of Amazon's KDP program and my reader base rose dramatically. My blog went from 10 visitors a week to over 100 a day and rising. I created book trailers, audio books and held seminars.

There were long hours, enormous amounts of work, constant disappointments, technical shortcomings, long periods of getting nowhere, and expensive advertising campaigns that didn't pan out.

However, slowly but surely, book sales improved. I received more hits to my blog, received more Twitter followers, more Linked-in endorsements, and more views on YouTube.

One last note. As writers, we often spend time in the world of our imagination. It's a great place to visit but don't start thinking you can live there.

Keep all your career decisions based in reality. If you've always aspired to be a romance novelist but your romance novels aren't selling but your wild west books are, well, you're a wild west writer so focus on that. You can always write romance novels as a hobby.

Remember that your readers will be loyal to you only for as long as you're loyal to them. Once you start generating some real sales, turn the marketing and sales over to companies that specialize in those things and spend your time creating new books and short stories and screenplays.

Read books outside your genre to learn new skills and methods that you can adapt into your own work.

Have as many friends as possible read your books before publishing them. I have often been amazed by some of the glaring errors I had made and still hadn't noticed after countless rewrites.

One glaring example was in my YA novel Half Moon Falls. In that book I referred to the same store by THREE different names. In the beginning it was the Storage Warehouse, midway the Storage Center and finally the Warehouse Center. Several of my writers' group members read the advance copy and didn't notice.

Fortunately, my editor did.

Everyone's story is different. We each have to follow our own path to become a success. Right now, having read this book you have all the tools you need to make it happen.

I'll see you on the bestseller list!

Thanks for reading. You can see more of my books at http://zackaryrichards.blogspot.com and at the Ari Publishing website http://aripublishing.com

The following websites are featured in this e book and are placed below for easy access.

For advertising products www.fiverr.com

Auto responder http://www.com/?421597

ISBN# https://www.myidentifiers.com/cart

Market Samurai Keyword software
http://marketsamurai.com/c/Zackary

Book covers
http://stockfresh.com/?affiliate=63510

To find booksellers in your area
http://www.local.com

To write Free ADS http://www.craigslist.com
http://www.USfreeads.com

To write articles http://www.goarticles.com
http://www.ezine.com

For marketing tips
http://www.bookmarket.com

For video software
http://www.nchsoftware.com/videopad/index.ht
ml?ref=4068062

For audio software
http://www.nch.com.au/wavepad/index.html?ref
=4068062

CPSIA information can be obtained
at www.ICGtesting.com
Printed in the USA
FFHW01n1326120718
47408705-50593FF